Sand in My Shoes

Katharine Ball Ripley

D0873206

DOWN HOME

Down Home Press
Asheboro, N.C.

Acknowledgements

The Moore County Historical Association is delighted to see Katharine Ball Ripley's *Sand in My Shoes* in print again. It extends appreciation to Jerry Bledsoe, publisher of Down Home Press, for presenting this as the first book in Down Home's Carolina Classics series. The association is grateful to Warren Ripley for his help and his excellent new introduction to his mother's book, as well as to Frieda Bruton and Jack Neill of the publication committee.

We would like to thank the following individuals who contributed generously to make this new edition possible: Mary Katherine and John Dozier; Dr. and Mrs. C.C. McLean; Jean and J.C. Robbins; Betty and Jack Neill; Marilynn and George Hoffman; Frances and Robert Mason; Sam and Marjorie Usher Ragan; Dr. Charlie and Marilyn Hartsell; Capt. Sherman and Ruth E. Betts; Dr. and Mrs. John L. Monroe; Katharine G. Taylor; Mr. and Mrs. Norris L. Hodgkins, Jr.; Mr. and Mrs. Charles P. Cole; Tim and Adrienne Ives; E. Earl Hubbard; Barbara and Clement Williams; Jack F. Carter, Jr.; Mrs. Watson G. Scott, Jr.; Mr. and Mrs. John A. McPhaul; Frank and Ann McNeill; The Country Bookshop; T. Clyde and Sally Watts Auman; Mr. and Mrs. Richard C. Yakel; Milton J. and Elaine M. Sills; Dr. David and Frieda Bruton; and in memory of Earl and Evelyn Bruton, who also grew peaches.

Finally, the rare perfect copy used for production of the new edition was loaned by a past president of the association and his wife, Mr. and Mrs. Harris Blake. It was given to him by his mother–in–law, Mrs. Louis A. Carter, postmistress of Jackson Springs, N.C., who knew well many of the people in the book.

—*The Moore County Historical Association*

Down Home Press
P.O. Box 4126
Asheboro, NC 27204

Introduction
to new edition

Katharine Ball Ripley was born at Charleston, South Carolina, March 20, 1898. Her mother, Fay Witte Ball, was a daughter of a highly successful Charleston banker. Her father, William Watts Ball of Laurens in the upcountry, had "read" law after graduating from college, then shifted to journalism. After a broad career, he was named editor of the *News and Courier* at Charleston where he remained until his death in 1952. He built a reputation as one of America's most outspoken newspaper editors in opposition to Roosevelt's New Deal.

Kattie inherited her father's ability to think on her feet as well as his courage, determination and drive. She also inherited his facility with a pen, his curiosity, and a willingness to try new ideas. She was often quite emotional, but never to the point of being maudlin.

She attended Converse College at Spartanburg. However, college began to pall when World War I brought thousands of officers to Camp Jackson near her parents' home in Columbia. Kattie had no intention of wasting time in college. Dances, parties awaited a popular girl. She was young. Life was to be lived.

She left Converse and returned to Columbia where she soon became engaged to Clements Ripley. Clem came from a long line of Vermonters. He graduated from Yale University where he was a member of the Yale Battalion, similar to modern ROTC. After earning an army commission, he was transferred to Camp Jackson where he met Kattie.

They were married in June, 1919, and a year later Clem, now a captain, was sent to Ohio on recruiting duty. A captain's pay proved far too small for adequate food and lodging for two people, one of whom was pregnant. Clem resigned his commission and looked around for a career.

His father came to the rescue with a $30,000 advance on his inheritance, big money in those days. However, it came with the provision that it be invested in a business—and his father picked the business. North Carolina peach farming, the fad of the day, seemed like a good occupation. It wasn't. Clem and Kattie gave it an honest try, but the peach boom broke. They lost their $30,000, but as Kattie tells it, they had a lot of fun and learned a valuable lesson: that life is a gamble. A sure, steady income may offer security but tends toward a dull life. Far better to throw the dice for a larger win.

During the years on the farm, Clem had been writing fiction, and the few sales he had made pointed to a new way of life. After enough checks came in to pay off the final debts on the farm, he and Kattie simply closed the door and walked out. They went to Charleston, where Kattie's parents were now living, and Clem set out to make a living with his pen.

Kattie also decided to try her hand at writing. She had turned out successful stories for school publications and had a certain flair for writing. She felt that her experiences on the farm were sufficiently entertaining to be marketable, and several editors agreed. *Sand in My Shoes* was published in 1931 and received dozens of favorable reviews. Six months later, it went into a second printing, and she decided to try a second book.

Sand Dollars, published in 1933, describes her life with Clem in Charleston during the Depression. They were broke, but just when they discovered that they could get along without material things, suddenly, for them, the Depression ended.

Throughout the lean months, Clem had been pounding his typewriter and brought in a few dollars with an occasional sale. Then a new novel, *Voodoo Moon*, sold to *Cosmopolitan* in 1933. It soon was published as a book under the title *Black Moon*, then was bought by Columbia Pictures. The movie, starring Jack Holt and Fay Wray, was released in 1934. The book established Clem as a writer. A steady stream of stories began to appear in magazines, books and movies. He also worked off and on as a contract writer for the Hollywood studios.

After *Sand Dollars* was published, Kattie turned out a novel, *Crowded House*, and three short stories, all in the early 1930s. She sold everything she ever wrote. Then she simply put down her pen and devoted her time to bridge, volunteer work and collaborating with Clem, mainly as critic. They would read his stories together, then decide on necessary changes. She had a remarkable sense of marketability. If a story made her cry, it would sell. If she could listen to it dry–eyed, it needed improvement.

Clem and Kattie were wrapped up in each other's lives, and when he died of cancer in 1954, much of Kattie's spark went with him. She kept up appearances, but life no longer held much interest. When her turn came a year later, also from cancer, she faced death with few qualms and probably genuine desire.

Sand in My Shoes covers only a few years, but it is a vital segment of Sandhills' history that should not be forgotten. The book may not be "politically correct" in every instance. However, her terms—"colored people," or "darkies"—were acceptable for the day and not intended to be derogatory.

Warren Ripley
Charleston, S.C.

1

We lived for seven years on a peach orchard at Samarcand, North Carolina.

A colored woman once said to me, "Why Aunt Holly, she's so ol' that befo' that ol' war — not this las' war, but that big war — she had white-folks." A quaint way of saying that white-folks had Aunt Holly, but the parallel is applicable to us and our farm. We hadn't been farming long before we found that the farm had us.

When we left the Army in 1921 we had a small capital and an intense disinclination to settling down to the usual life of business, golf and bridge of small-towners. A newspaper job in the city pays very little. The salary, plus our small income wouldn't be enough to enable us to live comfortably there.

There is something very enticing in the idea of farming to those who have never farmed and when we drifted down to the North Carolina Sandhills, we found there what seemed to be the ideal combination — a healthy outdoor occupation and plenty of social diversion, coupled with amazing profits. Grouped about Pinehurst at that time were perhaps fifty or a hundred peach orchards, many of them owned by people accustomed to living in town like ourselves, and all paying. Within the past few years the poor, almost worthless sand land, good only for growing pine trees and blackjack, had been found peculiarly suitable for peaches.

Northerners spending a winter in Pinehurst had bought land and planted orchards. Many of them had friends who, like us, were tired of the city and a safe five percent, and the little colony grew.

The orchardists led a pleasant life. They wore overalls through the day and bossed a gang in the fields and in the evening put on dinner coats and entered into the resort life of Pinehurst.

When Jim Boyd, since author of "Drums" and "Marching On," but then famous only as Master of the Moore County Hounds, took his pack through somebody's vineyard, the farmer in overalls, waving them on with the nozzle of his sprayer hose, was as likely to be someone you would meet at one of the university clubs as a native son of the soil.

It wasn't unusual for an orchard to pay for itself in

its first bearing season. Thirty percent on the investment after the first four unproductive years was considered conservative. Thirty percent, and three months'
holiday after the crop was gathered, was the slogan of
the peach-growers.

Raphael Pumpelly, the son of the geologist, had
the largest of all the North Carolina orchards. It was
said to have netted him eighty thousand dollars the
year before we came down. It was called Samarcand,
after the true Samarkand, but like everything else in
the Sandhills, the name had got twisted a little awry.

I first saw the place on a bright winter's morning —
a plantation store, a railroad shed, an enormous tin-
roofed packhouse, a peacock a-top a truck, spreading
his tail and admiring himself in the windshield, white-
washed cabins, rows of identical peach trees, red-
branched, stretching away between vistas of white sand
until they met in the blue haze of distance. Long-leaf
pines, blackjack, and at last the white frame house with
Amelie Pumpelly's formal garden planted with northern shrubs.

Amelie was a cousin of my husband's. There was a
log cabin which had been a sort of guest house and
schoolroom for the children. The Pumpellys offered
us the cabin as a temporary home.

Cousin Amelie gave a dinner and dance for us our
first week in the Sandhills. The dinner was small, only

(9)

about a dozen people, but at the dance afterward there were perhaps fifty couples, Pinehursters and peach-growers. Raphael had a very good dance hall above his plantation store. Sometimes he had music down from Washington and sometimes he had a string band of local darkies. There were darkies that night, jazzing it up. Huge lightwood fires flamed in the six-foot fireplaces. Of all woods, lightwood makes the most brilliant fire. There was peach brandy and scuppernong wine and corn liquor, all native products. It was a good party.

In front of the store, clear out to the road, the plantation hands, black and white, huddled in groups to watch the show. There were women dancing, some of whose dresses cost more than one of those men could make in a year. I felt myself then, as I was to feel myself so many times later on, as a sort of link between the rich people within and the very poor ones without. I found myself wondering what those countrymen thought of us — we who were dancing, which they consider is a damning sin, we women in our low-necked dresses, which they consider wanton. I was going to live, though I didn't realize it then, on the fringe of both their lives and never know either one entirely and never feel that I belonged to either.

But of course at that time I really didn't care what the country people thought. After all, I was dancing.

(10)

I wore a black velvet dress with a lace yoke and a Roman sash. It was a very *jeune fille* dress. I had been persuaded to buy it for my trousseau, because it was a Jenny model, though I longed to look old and sophisticated in those days. I am glad I didn't know then that it was to be my one winter dinner dress for six years. I remade it and changed it and remade it again, but I wore it until after our first big peach crop. There are compensations to wearing a dress that long. I can shut my eyes and see myself in the black velvet, and the long string of parties I wore it to comes back. The party where I drank too much, the party where I won twenty-five dollars at poker, and the party when the car broke down and we walked home three miles over the frozen road, and the party for Gloria Swanson — parties that we drove to so tired after a day fighting forest fire that I would sleep all the way over in the car, a dance when we got home after dawn in time to see the men start work in the fields.

I was wearing the black velvet when I came home from somewhere in the third year and found the nurse fast asleep and the baby delirious. We drove him a hundred and fifty miles that night to the baby specialist in Columbia. Three weeks later when I came back to Samarcand, the dress was lying on the floor where I dropped it when I took it off that night. It's easy to steam out the wrinkles in velvet, and it's surprisingly

(11)

easy for work and an interest in life to steam out the lines fear leaves on your mind.

Cousin Amelie's party was a great success so far as we were concerned. Clem and I had both seen enough of the people to be sure we should like our neighbors, and after talking to the peach-growers we were fired with enthusiasm for farming.

The peach-growers were the real people to us. Those who were merely wintering at Pinehurst were a sort of pale, nebulous background. Raphael introduced us first of all to the Maurices. Mr. Maurice had a quizzical, kindly face and was tall and lean and weather-beaten as a farmer should be, and she was lovely to look at and possessed of that cordial charm peculiar to certain Virginians that warms you straight down to your toes. I felt as though I had known Mrs. Maurice all my life from the moment she took my hand and said, " Amelie tells me you're really coming to live in the Sandhills. I'm so *glad* you're going to be one of us."

We sat near the blazing lightwood fire, watching the dancers sway in the flickering light, and the Maurices told me about their peach orchard between Pinehurst and Samarcand. They were keen about the country, their friends and their farm. They had come down several years before from the North, where Mr. Maurice had been a civil engineer.

They pointed out their daughter, Ellen. She was

about my age, and Mr. Maurice told me he had given her several acres of early peaches instead of an allowance and that she managed her crop herself. Right away I wanted to meet that girl and ask her a lot of questions.

We talked to men and women that night, to boys just out of college who had come down on a shoe string to make a fortune out of peaches, to young couples like ourselves, tired of the city, and to older men who considered peaches a business and a conservative investment. There was Mr. Butler, a charming, elderly man with a wide black ribbon tied to his glasses. He had seen most of the world and had chosen the Sandhills to live in. There was Sasha Jones and his wife, Ahlo, Sasha had been an engineer, a painter, a lawyer. There was something of the poet about him. He had an orchard and a vineyard near Southern Pines.

All of these people had something in common, from the young Birds, down from Boston only a month before and already the proud owners of a tract of sand land and a set of blue-prints, to Raphael himself, who had been one of the pioneer growers and had lived ten years in the Sandhills. They were happy people. They were confident of the future. They were having a lot of fun working their darkies in the fields, tinkering with their tractors, and climbing out of their overalls and into their dinner coats for a party at somebody's log

(13)

house or at Pinehurst in the evening after a day in the orchards.

Ralph Page, the son of Walter Hines Page, was then, and still is, the presiding genius of the Sandhills. He was the center of the party, the man who could make you stay and laugh some more when you were just struggling into your coat to go home. Ralph called the peach-growers the " county families " and the name stuck.

" So you like to ride," somebody said. " You must hunt with Jim Boyd's hounds at Southern Pines."

" Oh, do peach-growers have time to hunt, too? " I asked.

" That's the thing about this life," I was told. " You've time for everything. Stick around through the winter, work like the devil July and part of August during the crop, and swing on to the train north with the last crate of peaches for three months' holiday."

It was the dance that did it. I could see a long, low house with a terrace wall, and a saddle-bred horse, and me standing there ready to put my foot in the stirrup. Late summer afternoons, and Clem and me galloping down a sand road together, the way we had at Fort Sill. There were no gopher holes here, either, for a horse to break his leg in. . . . " Work in the fields." Roll the phrase around on your tongue. Doesn't it sound romantic? A pale yellow smock, a big sun-hat, and a

(14)

basket of red peaches worth — well, maybe not quite their weight in gold — swinging on my arm. We'd build a little house first, but one we could add to as we made more money.

And Clem! Clem had slips of paper covered with figures. All the orchards were paying amazing profits. A man he had talked to, Nat Hurd, from Pittsburgh, had bought a bearing orchard last year and paid for the whole thing out of his first crop. This was an unusual instance, perhaps, but peaches really were making money.

We talked a long time in front of the dying fire in the log cabin that night. Our capital was between twenty and twenty-seven thousand dollars. A bearing orchard of twenty-five or thirty acres (the smallest unit practicable for shipping car-lots) and a little house, would take all of it at once. We were not the gamblers then we became later. If we bought land and planted thirty acres and worked hard and lived cheaply for four years, until the orchard began to bear, at the end of that time although we should have invested all our capital, we could safely count on five thousand a year return at first, and later, when the trees were bigger, ten thousand or more. All about us people were doing it.

Everyone knows he can farm. Every man and every woman who ever came to our farm could tell us what they would do if it was theirs. Medicine is a mystery.

(15)

Law is a mystery. But I've never met a soul who didn't think he could farm. It seemed perfectly simple to us. We'd get a few suggestions from the more experienced growers, of course. We'd subscribe to farm magazines and study the government bulletins. We'd watch what the crowd were doing and learn from them.

We liked the people we had met. They seemed the happiest, most delightful group we had ever seen. We were reasonably convinced we should make money in farming — not a great fortune, but a comfortable living.

We were in love with our own mental conception of farm life.

2

The log cabin had been built for a toy. The windows had little yellow curtains with black cross-stitch children dancing across them. With a good temporary cook and an oil stove we were very happy. Raphael's dairyman did most of our marketing for us on his daily trip to Pinehurst, and the plantation supplied us with wood for our fireplaces. It gave us a feeling of pioneering to do without ice, but it was cold weather and we didn't miss it.

After a couple of months on the Samarcand plantation farming still seemed as simple to us as two times two. Clem went out every clear morning to work with the hands in Raphael's orchard. It was amusing to both of us at first to see him in overalls. It was the season for pruning the trees. Pruning isn't very hard physical work and it becomes absorbingly interesting as each tree, in spite of the effort to make it exactly like its fellows, has its own individuality. Clem used to come in pretty tired at night, but every day he was improving in his handling of the shears. He got a good coat of tan from the sun and wind and he was as proud of the callouses on his hands as a golfer is of his.

There was no responsibility attached to Clem's job. If he stayed out late at a party at night, when the plantation bell tolled dolefully next morning, all turning over and going back to sleep entailed was the loss of a day's pay. He wasn't working for the dollar and fifty cents a day, he was learning the business.

Listening to the pruners talk and retelling it afterwards was amusing. Many a Sandhills dinner party enjoyed black Cadger Barrett's explanation of all the troubles that beset fruit-growers.

" Yes suh, the Lawd done take a hate to them that grows fruits in the beginnin' of time. Ain't you recollec' in the Good Book when Cain bring in his offerin' of fruits to the Lawd? And the Lawd done frowned on Cain and he sent the fiah to Brother Abel's altar. The Lawd he don't want no fruits. He say ' Gimme meat.' Ain't do no good for Cain to git mad and bus' up Abel neither. The Lawd ain't never studied much 'bout them that grows fruits befo' or since. ' Man shall win his vittles by the sweat of his brow in spite of me,' said the Lawd."

The Samarcand plantation had always run smoothly

so far as we knew. But in the early spring, the busy time, Raphael had occasion to go to New York on business. Two days later, Noah MacAn, the superintendent, was kicked by a mule. It landed him in the hospital, and Cousin Amelie with the responsibility of the whole place on her shoulders came to Clem.

It was a sudden promotion from pruner to superintendent in charge of nearly a hundred hands. It was the time of the spring plowing. Every morning Clem had to get up in the cold dark in time to ring the farm bell so that the hands could be at work by sun-up. From that minute in the morning until night the working of the plantation was his responsibility. It was his first opportunity to see what an intricate business farming is.

The first day at noon it was the funny names in the time-book that he spoke of: Odessa, Rovesta and Digesta Johnson, and Little Lunch McNiel. But by that night it was a list of calamities.

Doc Caples, the driver of number one tractor, had burnt out a bearing. Doc incontinently disappeared and Mike McCrae, the plantation mechanic, acquired a "misery," that mysterious ailment which attacks colored people, particularly on working days. Clem wondered if, had Noah MacAn been there, Mike's misery wouldn't have waited until tomorrow. The fertilizer drills followed the tractor plow and a dozen hands waited idle while Clem struggled with the bearing.

(19)

Every day there was a new tale of woe. George, the barn man, took occasion to put into practice a cherished theory and fed the horses a wet mash when they came in hot from plowing. Clem and he nursed them with colic half through a long night.

The regular schedule for spraying the trees with poison dust hadn't allowed for a three-day windstorm. After the duster had gone into the orchard time after time only to be sent back on account of wind, and some two hundred dollars worth of dust had been blown into the next county, Clem asked Cadger, "Does the wind always blow this way in the spring?"

Cadger grinned and scratched his head thoughtfully. "Well, sir, I couldn't rightly say. Some time hit turn 'roun' and blow thataway."

The dust had to go out right away. The only time the wind died down was at night. They finally had to rig an automobile headlight on the duster and dust at night. Somebody had to go out with the darkies on the duster and generally that somebody was Clem.

There were other misadventures, some serious and some funny, but Clem wasn't in the mood to see the funny side. On one of the busiest days, Cousin Amelie sent up for a man and a mule to roll the tennis court. Clem sent her a darky, but after a few minutes the boy came back. "Mist' Ripley, Miz' 'Pelly say I put sacks onna mule's feets so he won' mark up the cou't.

But Mist' Ripley, ain' no mule in 'at barn want no sacks on he feets."

Lots of people have thought that an amusing story, but it probably cost Raphael at least twenty dollars in loss of time while Clem went up to see about the mule and the gang in the fields and fertilizer house idled. Anything out of the ordinary run of farm work is likely to make trouble. Clem discovered that in farming a day seldom works out as it is planned. Wind or weather or a darky funeral or some totally unexpected happening may throw the whole system out of gear.

At the end of about two weeks Noah came back and Clem turned over the time-book.

" I've learned one thing about farming," he told me. "There's a lot more to it than I thought. And I've learned one more thing — practically everything a darky does undirected is wrong. When we get our own place, we'll get a reliable white man."

When the orchards began to bloom the Sandhills had a clean, newly washed look. The Elbertas had deep-pink, tight little buds, and the Belles of Georgia had a ragged pink freshness like the pictures of a Japanese countryside. All through the winter in our spare time we had been driving about the country looking for possible locations for our farm. The beauty of the countryside gave a fresh impetus to our enthusiasm.

Raphael had great plans for Samarcand. Our young friends, the Birds, were already building a house and planting an orchard adjoining the plantation, and various other friends of Raphael's were considering coming down. Land was much cheaper at Samarcand than nearer Pinehurst. Farm labor was cheaper. And peaches ripened several days later there, which was better for the market.

In March we bought a farm, which adjoined Raphael's wild land, two and half miles from the highway and the plantation village.

It is hard to say why people accustomed to conveniences and the standardization of towns deliberately choose to go back into very much the same living conditions their grandparents had. But then, don't we call them the good old days? Maybe it's a desire for independence, an indefinite need of working our own problems out that some of us have, a resentment against monotony.

The farm we bought was an old one. There was a hundred acres, a barn and outbuildings, and a dwelling house which we planned to use for our farmer. The deed went all the way back to George III which should have given us pause, but didn't. People had lived on that farm since before the Revolution, and still the farm was so poor that, with buildings thrown in and at the peak of a land boom, we only paid forty dollars an acre

(22)

for it. In this respect it was no different from the other general farms of the section.

Clem, with the help of a surveyor and a gang of darkies, built the narrow sand road which leads to it from Samarcand.

We were to stay on in the log cabin for the present. Although there were few conveniences in the cabin, no electricity, no telephone, only wood fireplaces to heat it with, it was in the heart of a city compared with the isolated farm we had bought. And I was expecting a baby.

3

Warren Ripley was born in the log cabin at Samarcand on the 13th of April. It was a romantic idea of mine. I wanted him to be born in the country he was to grow up in, under very much the same conditions the people about him were born. Our neighbors, the Birds, were kind enough to drive to Pinehurst, sixteen miles, for the doctor.

I had never suffered any real pain in my life and I somehow couldn't make myself believe I ever should. There was something in the Bible — " A thousand shall fall at thy right hand but it shall not come nigh thee." I was literal and I was very young.

The cabin door stood open and the bright April sun flooded in. The nurse found Clem reading " The Jungle Book " upside down when she ran into the next room to tell him he had a son. They weighed him on the borrowed dairy scales, swung up in a diaper like the baby in the picture with the stork.

The afternoons are still short in April and as the hands came home from the fields at sundown they stopped by twos and threes to see the baby. The door was still open. The white men, always shyer than the blacks, passed by or stood and stared in at a respectful distance. But the colored women tip-toed in and peeped into the crib. They giggled and nudged each other and whispered, " Do Lawd, the purty li'l thing. I wish you well, Missus." There was such a stream of visitors I felt a little like royalty. Even Dusty, our English setter, came and dropped his wet nose over the crib-side to smell the baby.

He was a fat baby and his cheeks were puffed out the way a squirrel's are when he has a nut in each cheek. His eyes were tight shut and he waved his hands. His mouth sucked in and out like a fish's and altogether he was a most amusing person. I forgave him almost immediately for all the trouble he had caused me.

I have never quite made up my mind what I think of country women, whether I admire most their courage or pity their intelligence when I count their one, two, three — sometimes as many as sixteen head of children. Sanders, our farmer, once said to me, " Of course you can't expect to raise 'em all. You' bound to lose two-three."

When I look at country women, I am always glad Warren was born as he was and, paradoxically, that I do not live back in the time of our grandmothers as they do. Death seems to come closer in a cabin with no electricity, no telephone, no ether, than in a white hospital, but it seems more natural and less terrifying when you fight your own battle than when you submit yourself blindly to an anesthetic.

Our trained nurse, a city woman, was horrified with the whole affair. She was discontented in the country and I was not sorry to let her go after a little, as already we had to be careful about money for living expenses.

The baby and I went to South Carolina for a visit to my family.

When I came back to Samarcand, Clem greeted me with the news that I was just in time to hear the peach opera which Roger Derby had written. For weeks the county families had been rehearsing it. Nearly everyone had a part.

It was to be a sort of pre-harvest celebration, a eulogy of peaches, a symbol of the contentment of the community, a tribute to the goose that lays the golden egg.

" And I'm in the chorus," Clem said. " I'm a chorus man at last. We're peach hands. Want to hear our song? I'll sing it to you while I'm in the bathtub."

Even from Clem's rendition, with the accompani-

(26)

ment of running water, and many splashes, I recognized the tune as " We Sail the Ocean Blue " from *Pinafore*.

" We raise the Sandhills' peach,
    And our product is a beauty.
We are sober men and each
    Is attentive to his duty.
When the sun on the sand
Burns like a firebrand
    We stand to our hoes all day.
When a most welcome shower
Brings relief for an hour,
    We've plenty of time for play.
Oh boy! Oh boy! we've plenty of time for play."

" You should have been back for the rehearsals, Katti. This is a good crowd."

The party started off with an outdoor supper in the Pumpellys' garden. The cast and the few left to be audience were all there. Afterwards we trooped up to the dance hall above the store.

Mr. Butler was the hero of the piece, as he insisted he'd never found a worm in his orchard. The villainess was little Curculio, the peach worm. Jim Boyd was the engineer of the Peach Special. Nat Hurd, the Interstate Commerce Commission.

Somebody said, " The liquor's running short."

Jim Boyd said, " For God's sake, men, save it for the audience."

But the audience would have had a good time even dry, for the theme of the opera was a burlesque expression of the dream of the peach growing colony, the people who had come to live on the land and build up for themselves and their children a simple, farming community — who had found in peach growing a pleasanter, more satisfactory way to live than the life of struggle and competition of town.

Ralph Page's song, burlesque as it was, put it into words as nearly as a dream can be put into words —

" Oh, a Sandhills man is a soaring soul,
    As free as a mountain bird.
His note it should discount, up to any old amount,
    Secured just by his word.
He should make his home by his orchard's edge,
    And his cellar should be full of corn.
He should always sell his crop, at the market's very
        top,
    And be the happiest man e'er born."

" Clem, what a good time we're having," I said, as we walked back to the log cabin in the starlight. " Just think I've come home. The Sandhills is our real

(28)

home now." It was a new and pleasant thought, a safe, comforting thought.

We hummed the words of Ralph's song as we undressed.

" Oh a Sandhills man is a soaring soul,
        As free as a mountain bird."

We hummed it next day as we planned our new house.

Years later it was to drum through my head, a sad, shamefaced ghost tune, when '21 was referred to as the good old days.

A neighbor of ours had made sixteen hundred dollars net on one acre of honeydew melons last season.

His was the first experiment in our section. He was a Northerner totally inexperienced in farming, but he knew what he paid for a slice of honeydew in New York hotels.

He read up on melon culture and put in his crop. From then on the entire county had stood back and watched. After the seeds had been several days in the ground and no rain had come to wash them in and give them a chance to germinate, as the seed catalogue said they should, the grower stuck a post up in the midst of his fields. To this post he attached a little figure of St. Swithin, the patron saint of rain. Of course

(29)

he did it as a joke but it created a lot of comment among the country people.

That night the rain came. It poured like water from a faucet. The grower woke up and began to worry.

At three in the morning he got up, put on his clothes, sloshed out half a mile to his melon field and took St. Swithin down. The rain stopped by sun-up and there was no more for weeks. It made a deep impression on the neighborhood.

But Sanders, one of the pruners, was scornful. " Of course that's just foolishness," he said. " That there old idol couldn't have nothin' to do with bringin' rain."

He thought for a minute. " Now if you was to stick up a green snake on a post in a field, that'd bring rain. And it would bring the kind of rain you wanted, too, a drizzle drozzle that would fair pat the seeds in. I've seen it manys the time. But them Catholic idols they don't amount to nothin'."

St. Swithin or sound judgment or good luck, the grower had netted sixteen hundred dollars on his one acre.

That was last season. This year he had put in forty acres. We hadn't dared use enough capital to multiply sixteen hundred dollars by forty but we had decided we could have a small finger in the pie.

Our first venture in farming was the planting of

five acres of honeydew melons on a share-crop basis with Sanders. A share-crop is a crop raised on shares: that is, of the gross receipts stock and fertilizer take a third, land takes a third, and labor takes a third.

When I came back from South Carolina the melons were almost as big as oranges. We were very proud of them, each so round and perfect, growing on our own land.

4

Sanders was a painstaking soul, honest as daylight, and Clem, pruning with him day by day, had grown very fond of him. We had engaged him to be our farmer when we should plant our peach trees in the fall and felt quite altruistic in giving him this chance to make some real money out of the melons now instead of either starting him on his future salary of fifty dollars a month or paying him the current wages of two dollars a day for every day he worked.

He had an intense pride in his ability to do a day's work and a little over for his day's pay. I think it was a story he told about his experience in Fayetteville during the war that prompted Clem to engage him in the first place.

Sanders had been working as a carpenter on the cantonment.

" I didn't like it," he told Clem one day, "so I quit."

" What was the matter? Wasn't the pay good? "

" Best I ever got in my life. An' the work wasn't hard, neither."

" What was the matter then? "

" Well, they had 'em a steam engine down there with a whistle onto it. An' every mornin' when it was time to go to work, they'd blow it. Come noon, they'd blow it again. Nighttime they'd blow it again for us to quit. . . . Well, I know when to start work an' when to quit without nobody whistlin' at me. I ast the boss-man for my time an' I quit."

A Sandhills day begins at sun-up and ends at sun-down with an hour out at noon. I never knew Sanders, unless he was sick or his family were, to fail to make his day as long as he worked for us.

The Pinehurst people had gone north for the sum-mer. Only the peach-growers, who were busy with their crop, which was coming late in July, were left. We saw very little of our friends, there were no amusements, and the shops in Pinehurst were closed. We bought our groceries at the Samarcand plantation store. They had plain and fancy groceries, the fancy groceries being coca-cola and a cheap brand of sardines. The country people either sold or gave us what few vegetables we had. We had made the mistake of not planting a

(33)

garden of our own. Sandhillers plant cabbage and tur-
nips and squash and a few tomatoes. But what they
have, they share. More than once when I opened the
door in the morning I found a newspaper bundle or a
peach till full of vegetables, left by somebody, black
or white, on his way to the fields.

I raised a few chickens but we had no other meat.

We found some mushrooms in the sheep pasture
near the cabin. I looked them up in the encyclopedia.
We didn't know much about mushrooms, but they
had all the earmarks of an edible variety. Raphael's
dairyman said he'd never et this kind, but he'd
et another kind an' they et most as good as
squash. Sanders said he wouldn't eat no mushrooms
nor yet wouldn't drink milk from no cow that had
et mushrooms. We were hungry enough to take a
chance.

I stewed them in cream and we ate them on toast
for supper. They were delicious. There was a lot of the
cream sauce left, and I whistled for Dusty, our English
setter, who always adored anything with milk in it.
He sniffed at the pan and turned away. I dipped a
piece of bread in the liquid and tried him with that,
but he wasn't interested. A piece of dry bread had
fallen on the floor and he gobbled that up, showing
that he must be hungry for he generally didn't care very
much for dry bread. I had read somewhere that ani-

(34)

mals instinctively know when food is poison and refuse to eat it. I began to be a little worried.

Clem thought it was a joke, but I wasn't sure. I had heard somewhere that the first symptom of mushroom poisoning is drowsiness. Presently I looked up from a farm magazine I was reading and caught Clem in the middle of a big yawn. I yawned, myself.

Clem said, " Gee, I feel comfortable and sleepy. Let's go to bed."

It was about nine o'clock, which was our usual bedtime, but I began to believe we really were poisoned. Warren was a little tyke, about four months old. I wondered, if we died before morning, who'd find him and give him his breakfast. I went so far as to write out the formula for his milk and put it in an envelope addressed to Helen Bird, and left it on the mantelpiece.

Clem was so sleepy by this time that he had gone to bed, with the parting remark that one had to die sometime and at least he wouldn't have to do it on an empty stomach as he had done pretty nearly everything else this summer. I blew out the light, patted Dusty " good night " in the manner of one bidding a last farewell, and went to bed myself.

I fought against sleep for a long time, but after a while it sneaked up on me. Next morning we both woke up at daylight, the minute Warren began his

(35)

early morning yell. We had never felt better in our lives and we enjoyed mushrooms all through that summer.

A colored girl named Rose helped me in the cabin. All the Samarcand negroes were pressed into service in the orchard at this season, that being part of the contract under which they held their houses from Raphael, but Rose had attacked the plantation foreman with a hoe and he refused to work her. She was a powerful girl, slow-witted, but useful in washing dishes and diapers. She was devoted to Warren, and I always found her very docile. She couldn't learn to tell time, but if I had to leave Warren with her for a few hours I would set the alarm clock and she would give him his bottle when it went off.

Every day I drove over, Warren tucked into the seat of the Ford beside me, to watch our melons grow. By the middle of August they would be sold and we should have a net profit of a thousand dollars at the very least.

Most of the peach growers were planning to go north immediately after their crop was shipped. Many of the wives had gone already. They were going to Murray Bay or the Adirondacks or abroad, as usual. The weather was unbearably hot in August, my friends told me; a baby should have a change of air and the bracing northern summer. We counted on the melon

(36)

money to take us away. It seemed foolish not to spend it. Next year we'd plant forty acres and go abroad ourselves, perhaps. We were learning to be real farmers; it begins with optimism.

The first melon Clem brought home to me was prematurely ripened. It had a queer smell, too, and when we cut it open the taste reminded us vaguely of cucumbers.

Our neighbors told us that it was half cucumber, half melon. It is possible if cucumber seeds happen to be mixed with the melon seeds for the bees in carrying the pollen from vine to vine to cross them. We looked well over the patch. There were cuke-melons, and Texas cannonballs, and cantaloupe-honeydews, and a dozen other peculiar mixtures. We were soon connoisseurs on melons. We cut as many as a dozen at a meal to try, for of course there was no market for the off-varieties. We were alarmed. But our neighbors, both the countrymen who had farmed all their lives, and the peach-growers, some of whom had taken intensive courses at agricultural schools, consoled us. A waste of ten percent of a crop was nothing, they said. It was to be expected.

We deducted a little from our first estimate of net profit and continued to watch the true honeydews grow. Sanders sprayed and cultivated. I saw a minute hole occasionally in a melon; I noticed withered leaves

(37)

on several vines, but it was Sanders who at last opened my eyes.

" The pests is might' near eatin' 'em up," he said casually one hot noon. " But I aim to make better'n half a crop anyhow."

I couldn't believe him. Our beautiful green-gold melons, swelling in the sun. I must have looked foolish for he leaned back on his hoe and chuckled. He didn't seem worried.

" They'll bring a good price, what's left," he said. " Mist' Ripley, he's got education. A scholar like him'll know how to market 'em."

I asked Clem about it that night. I hoped Sanders' faith in him was justified and I secretly doubted if it was. But Clem was reassuring. He did know where to send them, he had ordered the crates (we still have half of those crates), he even had labels, and the Ford truck we had bought second hand was being made ready to do the hauling.

There was a thrill in packing that first five-acre crop of honeydews. Harvested, honeydews are the prettiest crop I know — big, pale, delicate yellow balls, warm with the field heat still in them, heavy and smelling deliciously with a weight and flavor they'll more than partially lose before they reach the shops.

Sanders and Clem and I picked and packed only ten crates the first day. We thumped them and lifted each

(38)

melon to test its weight before we broke the slender stem.

I think there is no joy in the world quite like the joy of something you produce yourself. We had gambled on land and seed and fertilizer. We had fought pests with spray and poison dust. We had prayed for rain and then frantically prayed that the rain would stop. While the melons were growing the weather had become vitally important. I never remember looking with any real interest at the sky before, or watching the sun rise except sleepily after a dance perhaps, but for the last few weeks I had waked at sunrise nearly every morning and breathed a sigh of relief if the sky was clear and pink. If we had been poetic (which we weren't) we might have been thankful that the honeydews taught us to appreciate the sunrise, and as I look back on it now, it seems absurd, but I almost believe that those clear, red suns, rising over the white sand and blue haze of pine trees and blackjack were worth it.

Our check for the first shipment of melons came back when we were well in the midst of shipping the rest of the crop. Honest Bill Parsons (self-styled) in Norfolk returned us ten dollars and two cents. We had expected at least forty dollars. Mr. Parsons had done his best but there was very little demand for honeydews just then in Norfolk.

It was a bitter blow. We tried other markets —

(39)

Washington, New York, Richmond. The same story. The market was glutted.

It was one of the commission men, a peach buyer who had come down to the near-by town of Candor, who gave us the answer. Our friend who had made the sixteen hundred dollars on one acre the season before had happened to hit a year when there were no cantaloupe on the market, due to a practically complete failure of that crop. Consequently any melon would sell at a fancy price and people would buy the more expensive honeydews. Our year there were plenty of cantaloupe. If the honeydews had come in in September, he said, it would have been a different story.

But why go on? We counted up everything. Excluding Clem's labor and mine we lost exactly three dollars and ten cents on our first venture in truck farming.

Sanders said, " That ain't so bad, Mist' Ripley. Heap o' folks does worse," which was true. Our friend with the forty acres, who had done everything on a very expensive scale, lost twenty thousand dollars and moved away.

Sanders's own third came to about fifty cents a day for his summer's work.

The excitement of the crop was over. August was hot. Rose killed a snake in the cabin bathroom and brought it in dangling on the end of a poker to show me. It wiggled and Warren laughed and held out his hands to catch it. We hurried the carpenters with the work on our house.

It was a long, one-story, white stucco house, rising from the white sand. It would cost six thousand dollars completed and you got quite a house for that in the Sandhills in '21. In the fall we would move in and plant the peach trees. Once on the land, where we would be always on the spot, farming would be simpler and certainly more profitable. The new house would be light and clean and carefully screened.

We moved in in the late fall and our real experiment in dirt farming began.

5

The new house was built under contract by a country carpenter named Sheffield. Sheffield and his darkies hated the sight of me with a wholesome hatred. A window would be put in at a curiously tilted angle. I would point it out and Sheffield would assure me vigorously that it was absolutely straight. I was always mean enough to hold up the plumb line and he would have to admit I was right — with a saving, "Don't see how it come to be that way, though."

We had had a New York architect draw up the plans and they were simple to follow. On the whole the work went well enough until the plumber arrived from Charlotte. The plumber came all prepared for a week-end in the country, with two gallons of corn liquor. He put in our simple bathroom and kitchen fixtures Friday and Saturday, but he stayed over Sunday to celebrate, and Sheffield celebrated with him. Monday morning when

Clem and I drove over to the farm the first thing we saw was Sheffield sitting on top of the water tank, singing away like a lark. It took until noon to get him down.

He was on one of those thorough country drunks. It was the first one I had ever seen, although later on I saw plenty of men with them, and I can readily understand why the members of the Women's Christian Temperance Union come mostly from that class. I've had to deal with labor once or twice in that condition, and it's very much like handling an over-wrought, nervous horse. It takes a quiet manner and a determined will. That's the trouble with most country women with a husband on a spree. They'll weep and they'll rant and they'll argue. You can't handle that kind of a drunk that way.

Sheffield's drunk lasted a week, and meantime the work on the house stopped. It was his loss, not ours, as he was building it under contract, but it was a nuisance to us as we were anxious to get it finished. On the sixth day he began to sober up. He counted his probable loss and felt very low in his mind.

Sanders told me about it. "Mist' Sheffield, he squatted on the ground above that there pit where they dug the sand from to mix the concrete. ' Sanders,' he says, 'it's the last straw. Mist' Ripley says I got to fill up this here pit.' I done told him, sure, he'd hev

(43)

it to do — we'd got no call to go fillin' it up. Mist' Sheffield, he says, ' Sanders, I'll give you a million dollars if you'll hit me on the head with yore ax an' bury me in this here pit.' I tol' him, ' Mist' Sheffield, you ain't got no million dollars.' Mist' Sheffield, he says, ' Sanders, all I got on me is fifty cents cash money. I'll give you that.' He just begged me to kill him, but I tol' him I wouldn't do it. Finally he says, ' D'you reckon Mist' Ripley'd kill me 'f I was to go over an' ask him to? ' I tol' him, ' I dunno if he'd do that, but the way he's feelin' he'd be mighty liable to hurt you some.' You won't believe me, Miz Ripley, but he bust out cryin' like a baby."

Sheffield had been on a typical country drunk. When a countryman drinks, that's what it means. He drinks until he's temporarily crazy.

Next morning he was shaky but in his right mind again. The building went on.

We left the log cabin to go over to our own farm in September. Clem and Sanders had already laid out the orchard and as soon as the dormant season set in the planting began — three thousand little whips, twenty feet apart each way, sticking straight up out of the sand.

The orchard surrounded the house on three sides and the forest hemmed the orchard in. The woods continued for I don't know how far back of us (I always supposed, for miles) with here and there a little clearing

(44)

and a farmhouse with a rutted wood road to lead into the Raleigh-Charlotte highway fifteen miles away.

We lived in the sand and our orchard grew in the sand, all except the lowest block of trees, but our farm land and farm buildings were in the red clay. The trees grew bigger in the clay, but the tractor bogged and the weeds throve. The wind blew the sand into the windows of our house and laid a fine powder over floors and furniture, but a half hour after a rain the road was hard and serviceable, which was why we chose the sand country to live in.

From any window in the house you could see the orchard rows stretching out to the woods beyond. The first year the little trees were just pliable switches whipped about in the wind. Unless it rained there was always a cloud of white dust in the orchard. The sand was so white and the sky so blue above, it gave the illusion that the sea (which was really two hundred miles or more away) must be just beyond the rise of the road. It used to make me restless for the water sometimes and give me a curious feeling of instability about the country, until someone told me that in some remote geologic period the whole Sandhills had been a huge inland sea.

Except for the wind and the noises the farm animals and machinery made, the farm was very still. Later on, after I had planted shrubs and the peach trees

(45)

had grown, we had lots of birds. But at first, either it was very, very quiet or it seemed so to me after the bustle of the big Samarcand plantation. I missed the monotonous, easy flow of the colored peoples' voices in the distance and their meaningless, effortless laughter. Sometimes I'd hear a Sanders baby's thin wail above the wind or Sanders hollering at a horse. But except for the noises my own household made, those were the only human sounds.

The colored people in the kitchen, more used to the stillness of the country than I, could hear a car coming a mile and a half away. After a while, I got in the habit of listening, and I could hear them, too.

The space, the isolation, and the quiet used to frighten me when we first moved over to the farm, but I got it all out of my system the first year.

There was one night when I was thoroughly afraid but after that I never locked a door or a window again, the whole time I lived at Samarcand.

It happened the spring after we moved in. Clem and Sanders and three white boys were pulling stumps. We had rented a stump-puller and were clearing five acres of woodland to plant dewberries on.

We had had no telephone at first, but since we knew we should need it for farm business during the coming summer we had indulged ourselves by putting one in a few days before. I have heard people in town compare

(46)

the telephone to a rattlesnake, coiled to spring, but it was such a luxury to us to have this connecting link with people after we had been without one for over a year that I ran to answer it with pleased anticipation every time it rang.

This morning it rang three rings, our number. I recognized the voice of the central at a near-by village. I knew she was very much excited by the way she said, " Hello, Miz Ripley," her words tumbling over one another as she went on — " Miz Ripley, I'm ringin' all the neighbors to tell 'em a terrible happening. There's a lady over near Tarville's been attacked by a colored feller an' they say he's headed for here. They want all the men to go out huntin' for him. You run tell Mist' Ripley, so's he can bring his men over here, an' they'll tell him which-a-way to go. . . . Miz Ripley, it's Miz McLagen, Jess McLagen's aunt from over 'bout Mizpah. She was down by the branch washin' her clothes an' the children was with her when he got her. They come a-runnin' home. . . . I got to ring up ev'body. Good-bye, Miz Ripley — you tell Mist' Ripley."

She didn't give me a chance to say a word or to ask a question, but I didn't need to ask. . . .

I wanted Clem to know about it. As I ploughed my way through the orchard, my shoes pulling me back and oozing sand at every step, I wondered how

(47)

many other women were hurrying to tell their husbands — the men who could do something about such an outrage.

A description of a lynching in a newspaper, the morning after it has happened, seems an almost unbelievable thing. In common with every decent Southerner I had been brought up to respect law and order and to feel that lynching is absolutely inexcusable. But as I ran across the orchard that morning the idea of shooting the nigger who had attacked Mrs. McLagen seemed as necessary and of as little account as shooting any other mad dog. To catch him quickly, to kill him violently, seemed the only thing that might give the woman a shred of her poor self-respect back.

I had read enough and heard enough of rape, that terror of Southern women on lonely farms, in a childhood spent in the South, to picture the whole thing. I didn't know Mrs. McLagen, but that didn't matter. It might just as well have been Mrs. Sanders or it might have been any poor woman alone. A patient, unsuspecting farm-wife, bent over scrubbing her clothes in the branch — a black, lust-crazed beast peeping at her through the bushes, creeping stealthily on her — his black hands crushing her throat to keep her from crying out — the little children screaming, frightened out of their wits, running towards their father working in his cotton patch. Could she ever hold up her head and

(48)

face her husband and friends again? Was she injured? Maybe she was dying!

Clem dropped the big chain as I came up. I was out of breath with excitement and running. I called him aside. . . . I was pretty well carried away with my horror story and Clem tells me now that I was very dramatic — gestures and all.

Clem looked at the mules working the stump-puller and at the three men (two dollars per man per day).

" I won't get the vines in for another week as it is," he said. " If Mrs. Morgan telephoned everybody she said, they won't need us."

I was amazed. I argued. . . . But I'm not much good at arguing — I'm better at telling people. I pointed out that in North Carolina a Vermonter ought to act like a North Carolinian.

" Let the sheriff do it," said Clem. Then he added, " To tell you the honest truth, I wouldn't go anyway. If they catch that poor devil, somebody'll be fool enough to have the idea of lynching him. I couldn't stop it and I won't be mixed up in it."

So that was that. Clem went back to the puller, and the mules tugged away and the chain creaked.

But my heart still burned with sympathy for Mrs. McLagen. As I turned back I saw a country woman, from whom I sometimes bought eggs, hurrying up the

(49)

road to my house. Her mild, blue eyes were snapping with excitement. I never knew how she had found out about the rape, since I knew she had no telephone, but she had heard all the details and was anxious to share them — a rare thing in a Sandhills woman.

I recognized in her at once a sister with a sympathetic Southern viewpoint.

" You heard about Miz McLagen, I reckon! " she called before she reached me. " Ain't it a terrible thing? . . . Miz Ripley, she met that colored feller down at the branch an' she was passin' the time of day with him just as clever as I'm talkin' to you here. An' he took an' done her that-a-way! "

I knew that by " clever " she meant " pleasant " but there was something in the way she accented the word that caught my attention. I could feel that she was bursting with gossip that she scarcely dared put into words.

I said, on impulse, " Do you mean, maybe Mrs. McLagen — well, encouraged the boy by being pleasant to him? " The thought startled me almost as much as the news of the rape had done.

One glance at her face told me that the cat was out of the bag.

She hesitated. She twisted her sun-bonnet string. She said slowly, " Miz McLagen was more'n a mite crazy. . . . Al Belk's oldest girl, she was, an' a wild one when Joe McLagen married her."

(50)

It was a totally new thought to me. I knew, of course, of the half-witted white girl near Samarcand, who rumor said, had had a mulatto baby. But the idea that Mrs. McLagen possibly — rather probably — had encouraged a negro boy and then accused him of rape with all its horrid consequences was revolting to an extreme. I felt utterly futile and ashamed. I, who a few minutes before would have cried them on to the man-hunt, even with the probability of lynching at the end of it! These rural, back-woods people had complexities that I had never dreamed of. I had come up against something about which I didn't know enough even to reason the right and wrong. By the side of this woman I was just ignorant and foolish. I was glad Clem had had his stumps to pull.

I wanted to forget the whole affair. I didn't want to think of the morbid, tortuous ways a woman must tread who would do such a thing. I just wanted to forget the incident. But it was to have a queer aftermath for me.

That afternoon, they finished with the stump-puller and Clem and Sanders drove off on the truck with it, Mrs. Sanders and the children crowded in the back. They were to be dropped in the village to enjoy the excitement while Clem and Sanders drove on to return the stump-puller.

After supper, I called Rose, the colored girl, but got no answer. Her little house, which stood just beyond

(51)

the kitchen, was dark. I remembered hearing somewhere that when there's trouble over a darky all the
other darkies mysteriously disappear.

I told myself it was a coincidence. Rose often walked
over to Samarcand after supper and returned at sun-up,
but I would have kept her with me this night, with
Clem away. Warren was only a year old and fast
asleep. I locked up the house carefully and put a lamp
on the telephone table, intending to telephone the Birds
for company. They were our most intimate friends and
their orchard lay only two miles away.

I rang several times, but the 'phone was dead. Pre-
sumably Mrs. Morgan had left the exchange to enjoy
the village excitement. Opposite me was a window. Through it I could see the outside angle of the
kitchen wall, and a light still burning in the kitchen
window.

I got up, intent on saving kerosene. I could see, too,
our Ford, standing in the driveway, and I took a step
towards the door with the idea that I would put it in
the shed. Then I remembered that the self-starter was
broken and I couldn't crank it. It was moonlight outside and I was thinking that was lucky as it wouldn't
rain on it, when I saw, or imagined I saw, the shadow of
a man leaning against the running board.

On the instant I blew out the light — I don't know
why, for a second later I was feeling around for matches.

(52)

I told myself what an idiot I was, and I struck a match and lit the lamp again. My fingers were trembling.

I took the lamp into the living room and sat down with a magazine.

I kept making excuses to myself about the kitchen lamp. I thought maybe I'd get a glass of milk later on and I'd need it. I thought, "Anyway, kerosene's cheap. . . . Read and forget about him, you fool," I told myself. "Probably he'll go away."

I made myself read on and was doing nicely and had pretty well got my nerve back, when I heard a low whistle.

There was no mistake, and I knew it wasn't a bird. Somebody was whistling near the kitchen door. There I was, sitting in the bright light.

I sat as still as I could and kept my eyes on my lap. I could hear steps softly crunching in the sand. He may have whistled again; I don't remember. But I do remember hearing the gentle rattling of the kitchen window, and I couldn't make myself sit still any longer. It didn't occur to me that it might not even be a colored man. I knew it was, and I knew which one it was. I never doubted that it was the boy who was being hunted.

I didn't want to scream, but I felt that I must run somewhere very fast. Two miles away from anybody with that man outside! I hope I'm not an unnatural mother, but I know I did an unnatural thing that night. In that minute of terror I forgot I had a baby. I just thought of me.

I jumped up. I ran to the door and opened it, and called out, not loud, but as firmly as I could:

"George!" I called, with a sort of subconscious memory of Pullman porters. "George!"

Nobody answered, of course. But once I had started, I had to go on. I walked deliberately towards the car and I called again.

"Come here, you, boy!" I said. "Come here and crank my car."

And out of the shadow of the kitchen steps he came. He was tall and a little sullen, but he obeyed the voice of authority and cranked.

When the engine was running and I had my foot on the throttle, I felt lots better. "What are you doing here, boy?" I demanded.

And of all answers, his was the most natural, and to me in my state of nerves, the least expected. . . . "Lookin' for Rose, ma'm," he said. "I'm Li'l Lunch McNiel."

The light burning low in the kitchen window — Of course he thought Rose was probably asleep in a kitchen chair. I was weak with relief. Of course I knew Li'l Lunch. Many a time he had helped haul wood for us at Samarcand. I let him stand on the running board until I made the turn to the Birds'. I looked back and saw him trudging on towards the plantation.

The Birds were in bed but they got up and came over and sat with me until Clem got home. Warren was still asleep.

They caught the boy who did the rape twenty miles away that same night. He was walking down the railroad track and he surrendered to the sheriff. He was only eighteen years old. He was later convicted and, I suppose, duly electrocuted.

Mrs. McLagen left our neighborhood. Mrs. Sanders told me her kinfolk urged her to go. Her uncle even foreclosed the mortgage which he held on their little farm. But I got rid of the fear of being alone in the country once, and, I hope, for all. If you are isolated in the country anything may happen but probably won't. There's no use worrying about something you can't help. Clem bought me a pistol, but I hate loud noises so I never even once fired it, and in a little while, when Warren learned to walk, I locked it in a box and put it on a high shelf.

I found it there, covered with dust, years afterwards.

6

I had a colored couple the first winter in the new house. They were both field hands, and the man was not only unused to housework of any sort, but felt it beneath him. Cutting firewood, sweeping and the like were women's work. I was inexperienced. I didn't know how to control him, or, to use the local phrase, to get the work out of him. He hibernated in a spilt-bottomed chair in front of the kitchen stove. Lily, his wife, was willing and obedient but almost as stupid as Rose had been. I taught myself to be a very good cook in my efforts to teach her. She was fond of Warren, and was always good to him and very patient.

I was so busy those first few months with the baby and housekeeping that I knew what went on on the farm only in a vague way. When milk comes twice a day in a pail and must be set to rise for cream, which in turn is made into butter, the details of housekeeping take much more time than when the milkman brings milk in a bottle and butter in a box to your door. Oil lamps that have to be cleaned and filled are very different from pressing a button for light. An eighteen-mile drive to Pinehurst for supplies twice a week is more difficult than a telephone call to the butcher and grocer.

Our standards were different and our living conditions were of necessity quite different from the usual Sandhills farmer's. We couldn't bring ourselves to eat in the kitchen, which was warm and comfortable, but shivered in the draughty dining room. A fire was kept up all day in the living room, which meant that every hour someone must remind Lily or Leo to fetch wood. Often I got it myself. We had to be a bit frugal with wood even then. It was fairly expensive to cut and haul from the woodlot for one thing, and Sanders was busy and couldn't be spared for another. We were sparing with water for the same reason. Once a week Clem or Sanders pumped the tank full, and what with one thing or another going wrong with the gasoline engine, it generally took all day.

But the house was new and the baby was new and all the little difficulties were fun that first year.

We saw a good deal of the Pinehurst people, the Northerners who had winter cottages there and who came down with their children, their pet dogs, and their white maids, for the golf or polo. We drove over to

(57)

dinners and parties two or three times a week. Clem played polo. It was cheap, as polo was new at Pinehurst and they needed men to fill in and to exercise the ponies.

The colony of peach-growers had plenty of servants and plenty of leisure, too. They had comfortable, big houses for entertaining and except for the pruning there is very little to do in the orchards in the winter. That year the growers amused themselves counting up the fat profits they would have in the summer. They were justified in doing it in the light of past performances.

There was a good crowd about our age and we had a lot of fun together. Some of them grew peaches and some of them just resorted. Everybody got together and gave a series of masquerade dances in Raphael's hall at Samarcand. Some of the crowd ordered their costumes from New York. Others had gorgeous fancy-dress costumes they had worn at more elaborate masquerades at other places. But we and the Birds and some others used to have a lot of fun getting our costumes together out of whatever we could find. We would wait until about an hour before the dance and then begin to think about something to wear. Once I let down my hair, rolled down my stockings, cut off the hem of my skirt, and went as a little girl. It was as long ago as that.

Another time we raided the Samarcand store for overalls and red cotton handkerchiefs to go as field hands,

(58)

and Milton Bird produced the *chef d'œuvre,* a derby hat and a pair of spats to wear with his, and went as a gentleman farmer. Once we dressed Clem up in a plaid automobile rug, and with the hot water bottle for a sporran, he went as a Scotchman.

After the dances people would sometimes drive over to our house for eggs and coffee. Often after we were in bed someone would come to borrow an overcoat or a little gasoline. Once I woke up with the glare of a flashlight in my eyes. I could just make out a stocky figure all in bright green. It was Tony Bryan, representing the Irish Free State.

" For God's sake," he said, " lend me a couple of gallons of gas and a quart of corn. I've got the orchestra in my car, three miles down the road, and they're stuck."

We had an awfully good time that winter.

When spring came there was much more to do on the farm. So far we had spent approximately fourteen thousand dollars on the place, which was considerably more than we had intended it should cost us to date. Roughly, four thousand had gone to buy the land, six thousand had gone into building the house, and the other four thousand had been spent for clearing the land, planting the trees, labor, and equipment.

We had allowed ourselves two hundred a month to live on and we had kept within it. But the total for living expenses had cut our capital another twenty-four hundred.

We figured it out just a year after we had bought the farm, and we referred to the budget we had made in the first few weeks after we had come to North Carolina. There was no one item that was particularly more than we had estimated, but each one seemed to have taken a little more money. The well for the water supply, for instance: instead of digging thirty feet, we had found that by the nature of our land, to avoid surface water, we had to drill a hundred feet. We had reconsidered our first allotment of fertilizer for the young trees and to those which were planted on the old, worn-out farm land we had given a double allowance. In buying a pair of mules Clem had picked out heavy ones. Sand land is light and a comparatively small horse or mule can cultivate it, but we had needed the heavy pair for pulling the stump-puller and clearing. Our feed bills had gone up in consequence. Since only thirty acres of our land was in peaches, and five in dewberries, we still had enough cleared clay land to have made our feed. But our first year that was one of the things we hadn't time for. We had bought the farm late for putting in feed crops, such as oats and hay, and although Sanders had pointed out that " feed do run to a sight of money when you have it to buy," we had felt it would be far better to concentrate on the honeydews.

(60)

In one way or another something over sixteen thousand dollars had gone.

We faced the fact after a year on the farm that we'd have to spread our capital very thin if it was to last until the trees bore. 1921 had been another good peach year, both for the size of the crop and in the prices paid for it. We were confident that all we had to do was to make a crop to be sitting pretty.

We had to economize carefully on our living. Two hundred dollars doesn't go far when the car alone costs fifty dollars a month to own and run. Our darky servants came to another fifty, which left a hundred dollars for food and clothes and all other incidentals.

The car was a necessity. It was our only means of communication. We used it for marketing in Pinehurst. We drove to Samarcand every day for mail. Even if we could have gone entirely without friends and diversion we had to have a car to keep in touch with the other growers. For instance, the growers had a new (their first) coöperative association, and Clem attended the meetings at Aberdeen, twenty-five miles away, to pick up what he could of the marketing end of the business before our first crop should come in. Farm machinery is continually breaking down and we were always having to drive over to Candor for parts. We discarded the idea of doing without a car as impractical.

As for the servants, we simply didn't want to do

(61)

without them. I tried it for six weeks and my housework took every minute of my time, and even so I had to call on Clem to chop and bring in wood and do a good many other things.

I should like to bring out here that in moving to the country we were not primarily interested in making a fortune. We knew we should never be rich, though we expected to make a comfortable living. What we were looking for was life — a system of living. We wanted freedom from the standardization of towns with its drive of social and economic competition. We knew we should have lean years. We knew we should have to work hard. We expected to have to give up many of the luxuries that had become necessities in the city. But at no time did we expect, or were we willing, to sink into the living conditions of the poor whites. I doubt if anyone deliberately steps down from one standard of living to a much lower one.

We enjoyed the country. Clem would put in his day with the stump-puller and come in dog-tired but enthusiastic at night to go to bed at nine o'clock. But he couldn't sleep in his overalls and he wanted sheets on his bed. Sanders never owned a pair of pajamas or even a nightshirt in his life. My housekeeping was several times as elaborate as Mrs. Sanders' and several times harder work. My baby had to have a bath every day, and a regular nap, and carefully prepared food at regu-

(62)

lar intervals. The little Sanderses gnawed on sweet potatoes when they got hungry and in spite of the baby books I lent Mrs. Sanders to read she insisted on believing it was her Fundamentalist God's will that they be undersized and colorless. Clem and I, ourselves, couldn't live on a diet which consisted wholly of fat-back, soggy cornbread, and sweet potatoes, day in and day out, with an occasional variation of " greens," as the Sanderses did. Nor were we willing to all dip into the same dish together as they did.

We wanted baths and clean clothes after the day was over, and time to read and talk. We kept the servants and did without radios and victrolas, and I spent my days out-of-doors, poking into this or that on the farm. I place it as one of the few wise decisions I ever made. It was an investment for me in health and enjoyment, and strangely enough, in the long run it paid cash dividends. If I had simply become a household drudge through those first years, I should never have learned enough about peaches to be any help in the crop later on.

We had between eleven and twelve thousand dollars left and the orchard wouldn't come in for three more years. We didn't dare allow less than six thousand dollars for the orchard — and that was a close allowance. We paid Sanders alone six hundred dollars a year. That left us less than a hundred and seventy dollars a month to live on, and we had just barely been getting along on two hundred as it was.

Well then, we had to have more money — a money crop. We had five acres of dewberries coming along. They were year-old vines, but with luck we might net five hundred dollars this year. We still had ten acres of cleared land. On the theory of " if at first you don't succeed . . ." Clem put the ten acres into honeydews.

Five acres last year had failed, but every year is a new year. We had learned how to combat the pests of last season. We knew what time to plant so as to miss the canteloupe crop. We got the seeds from a different seedsman and prayed that they would be true to variety this time. We had had experience in handling and packing them.

But our ten acres of honeydews was practically a complete loss. A new disease, to us at least (a form of wilt) attacked the leaves. We wrote the Bureau of Agriculture for information — and got it eight months later.

Meanwhile we went after it with Bordeaux mixture, which is a good general spray. It was a rainy summer. Generally the sun blazed down in the Sandhills, but this summer he showed his face so seldom that the people back of us, in the clay country, a lot of whom insist on going on mean solar time (God's time), hardly saw him often enough to keep their clocks set right. It

(64)

rained and rained. The rain washed the spray off the melon vines, and the rain spread the wilt.

To add to our troubles, a brand new pest, a melon borer, attacked the melons from the underside. There was no way to get at him without lifting each anæmic little melon. We lifted hundreds of them and hardly ten percent were without a tiny puncture. There was not enough of a crop left to be worth shipping.

What few there were we picked anyway and had them hawked around in the truck, but it didn't pay. We hardly got the price of the seeds and fertilizer out of the honeydews.

In spite of the weather, we made a small dewberry crop. We engaged a few women and a dozen colored children to pick them. Clem or I sat all day in the makeshift packhouse under a roof of green blackjack branches and solemnly paid a cent a till each time a small child appeared with a tray of six. We had a big bag of pennies. The children liked to get their pennies in their hands each time they had picked a trayful. It kept them interested and they would work all day. We tried paying them in a lump at the end of the day but it didn't work. A day seems infinitely long to a darky child, and without the stimulus of the present penny he loses interest and runs away to do something else. In dewberry time it's the owner who pays and pays.

We had hoped to make four or five hundred dollars

on the project, but with the bad season we were thankful to net a little over a hundred.

Lily and Leo had gone (as now there were no fires to build, I really didn't need both of them) and Rose was back with me. She and I put up dozens of jars of preserves, some of which I sold, and Sanders and I made such excellent dewberry wine that Sanders, himself a teetotaler, told me with honest pride, " Done kep' my uncle drunk a week on it."

Summer nights, with the moon rising up from be-hind the rim of the orchard, making the white sand as light as snow, Clem and I used to sit on the terrace wall and talk about money. It wasn't of the future we talked — we had no doubts of the future. It was of the years between and our immediate needs. We juggled our accounts about. We charged the cow to the farm and let it support her for the manure. We called the milk the by-product. But it was borrowing from Peter to pay Paul, and in the end the farm expenses always had to come first. The baby might need a bigger crib, but the orchard had to have a new harrow.

We could have sold the place that summer, I think, and got our capital back. All we would have lost was a year's work. But it never occurred to us to sell it. We and all the growers about us were confident of the con-tinued profits from peaches. At that time, many suc-cessful men who had made their own fortunes were buying or planting orchards. Some of these men had no idea of living on the farms. They put in superintendents. The orchards were simply business propositions expected to pay.

Every day we would look out at our little trees. The little peach switches of last summer were three-branched bushes with twigs and leaves now.

Three years from now, I counted — three thousand trees yielding half a crate a tree, at last year's price of three dollars a crate, makes forty-five hundred dollars. The year after, a crate a tree makes nine thousand. And the year after that, maybe two crates.

Pleasant daydreams for a summer's day.

7

When the peach season came, Clem went over to work for Raphael. He would have gone for the experience alone, but when Charlie Bennet, Raphael's superintendent, offered him a job selling culls at four dollars a day he was darn glad to get it.

Raphael had put grading machinery in the packhouse for the first time that year and the machine wasn't quite adjusted right and pinched the peaches, making lots of seconds. Any peach with a blemish is a cull. Clem and a couple of boys sold as many as a thousand bushels a day to trucks who peddled them to near-by cities. Hundreds of people drove down to buy a bushel or two and see the packhouse at work.

I used to go over, the first day to eat peaches, after that to watch the packers.

The packers are mostly Florida and Georgia professionals. In the winter they pack oranges and tomatoes, then follow the fruit north to the Georgia and North Carolina peach crops. They go on into Virginia and New Jersey and are likely to wind up in the fall in Michigan packing apples.

They wore white shirts and duck trousers, their hair slicked back with pomade and a hunk of gum in their cheeks. Their hands flew with the precision of an expert typist's.

The machinery whirred. One by one, two by two, by dozens the peaches rolled slowly along the belt, past the bright-cheeked North Carolina girls, who graded out the defective ones, to be sized by the machine and dropped into the bins.

Right hand — left hand — color side up — each peach kissing, but not pressing, its neighbor in the till. I watched the packers' deft hands, and I learned the packs — a two-three, and a two-two, and a two-one, and the tricky eight-seven-eight that the commission men frown on, long before I ever fitted a peach in with my own hands.

Day after day and all day long the wagons creaked up to the packhouse and unloaded full picking baskets until the floors sagged with the weight. Sometimes I could see a gang of seventy-five to a hundred darky girls, picking down the rows. This one is ready to come and that one won't be ready 'til tomorrow — plop, they go in the baskets. Mike is a sort of *comprador* (stud-horse,

(69)

is the Sandhills term). He's a big, black buck darky with a drum. The girls won't sing " reel-tunes " but they all sing when Mike beats out, " Jesus Chris', He done it all," in ragtime. Strutting it out, hips and elbows swinging —

> " Jesus Chris', He done it all,
>   He done save' me from de fall.
>   Such a feelin' in mah breas' —
>   Ah got perfec' peace an' res',
>   An' Jesus Chris' (*boom, boom*) He done it all."

The peaches fall like hail, and Charley Lewis, the picking foreman, yells from row to row, " You there — drop 'em easy! Like aigs."

But all the time, the wagons keep creaking up with their loads. About the time the tired sun goes down the special chugs up to pick up the cars. Each peach fitted in its till, each till in its crate, each crate labeled and fitted in beside its neighbor. Ice in the bunkers. The cars roll.

The culls that were left, hundreds of baskets of them sometimes, stood on one end of the platform. We used to stand among the baskets, ankle deep in spilled peaches, the smell of ripe peaches everywhere, the fuzz prickling our arms and necks and faces, sometimes even the small of my back, with an agonizing tickling. The gnats swarmed.

(70)

We had to dump the leftovers to make room for to-morrow's supply. Raphael had a herd of hogs and they fed the culls to them. About the fifth day, the hogs struck and Charlie Bennet, the superintendent, had a big grave dug and they dumped the culls in that.

Late one afternoon a long, lean fellow in dingy over-alls came into the packhouse. Business had been dull, and Clem was sitting on an overturned peach basket with a pad of paper on his knee, writing. He put it down to ask the conventional, " What can I do for you? "

The man hesitated and shifted his quid. He spat, and got good distance, too, even for a Sandhiller. He picked up a peach, broke it in half, looked disparagingly at the halves, and tossed them on the sand beyond the packhouse. Most cull-buyers do this, but it is a mad-dening trick, as all the peelings and pieces of peach must be picked up to keep them from spreading worms and brown rot to next year's crop.

" What's your best price on a few bushels o' peaches for cannin' purposes? " he drawled.

Clem told him, fifty cents a bushel.

" Cap," said the man after a hasty glance around, " Make me a better price'n that. . . . Will y' have a li'l drink? " He pulled his faded blue coat a little aside to show a pint whiskey flask.

It took us a moment to understand. It was our first

(71)

introduction to a moonshiner. We had always wanted to meet a moonshiner. I smiled at him and he wiped his hand on his overalls and held it out.

I stayed with the culls, while Clem and the moonshiner slipped into one of the iced cars for that little drink. When they came back in a few minutes Clem told me in a whisper, " It's all set."

We were all three very diplomatic. We had a little talk, very guarded, in which we referred to the man who was to make the brandy as a friend of Our Friend. It's always done that way. It's the correct thing in moonshining circles. The moonshiner said, " I — I mean, my friend has to take a sight of resk to make this here licker." He said, " I — that is, my friend, ain't got no call towards that chain-gang at Atlanta."

Any kind of a cull will make good brandy. We got Charlie Bennet to sell us a truck load of the softest ones cheap. That night Clem and I drove sixty bushels down a rutted road to an old shed which stood on a disused farm. Two men, both long and lanky, and one unmistakably Our Friend, stood in the shadow of the shed.

" Walk down the road a piece an' stand with yore back turned," whispered Our Friend in a voice he was obviously trying to disguise.

We did as we were told, but they couldn't see us fifty feet away, so I turned around and looked back. The two shadowy figures unloaded the baskets, dumped the peaches in the shed, and threw the empties back on the truck. At a low whistle and a cautious, " All right! " we came back to the deserted truck, climbed up, and drove off.

We were to have a third of the brandy, the moonshiner, two thirds. Unfortunately the still was raided by the sheriff and while Our Friend got away, we got no brandy.

Charlie Bennet, the superintendent, summed up the situation. " Well, it mostly happens like that," he told me. He went on, slowly, " I recollect I went in cahoots with a fellow one time to make some brandy."

" How'd you come out? " I asked.

" Fifty-fifty. He got the brandy an' I got the cahoots."

I learned afterwards that the usual arrangement for going into the moonshining business on a large scale is this:

The silent partner guarantees the maker's bond. The moonshiner, it is understood, skips his bond if he is caught. When you consider it, it is really a very reasonable plan, too. The difficulty is that the silent partner is at the mercy of the moonshiner, who can cheat the eye-teeth out of him if he has a mind to, by simply selling the stuff and refusing to pay up — which is probably what happened to Charlie.

At the end of the peach season, Clem had coming

(73)

to him a check for his time. But he had besides, the story he had been scribbling, sitting on the overturned basket among the soft peaches. It had to do with two red-blooded adventurers, starving to death in the desert. A month later he sold it to a magazine for a hundred and ten dollars.

It was his first sale. No check has ever looked so big since. Clem said, "Great God, I've learned something. The pen is lighter than the pick."

But I felt as I think the canary must when you open the door of his cage. Maybe he doesn't want to fly out. Maybe he likes the cage better than the outside. But the door is open. He doesn't have to stay unless he wants to.

It wasn't enough to take us North with the peach-growers, but we decided to leave the sand and the heat and the vegetable garden where no vegetables grew, and drive down to the coast and swim off the peach fuzz and forget the farm for a week.

8

"Let's go to the coast," said Katharine and Clements.

"Let's go to the coast," said Warren alone.

It was a silly parody on a child's verse, but we sang it at intervals all the way as we rattled in our Ford across North Carolina.

Long stretches of pine and scrub oak, with here and there an unpainted, flimsy farmhouse on stilts. Log cabins with pink grindstone chimneys — red clay — red-cheeked children — faded women — long, lean, flat-chested men. Three small boys with such flaming red heads and such broad Scotch accents when we asked road directions it seemed strange to see them in overalls instead of kilts. The little towns with their Scotch and English names — Lillington, Dunn, Kingston, Dover.

In every town there is the King's House. Even Warren learned to point them out. In the littlest towns it rises grandly above its neighbors, a monument, usually to the year cotton went to forty cents. Clapboards with huge, white columns and a pergola — sometimes even a fountain. Red brick, carefully copied from pictures in the brick catalogue, built square to the highway, with all the trees cut down and a few definitely placed ornamental shrubs. Once (we were delighted) a Moorish mosque with a pink-and-green roof and a minaret. In the older towns the King's House is generally Victorian — dingy with a faded grandeur of cupola and bay windows. But next door, or across the road, there is always the Crown Prince's home, very new and obviously a composite of all the Crown Prince saw in other houses on his visits to the cities. We saw Kings in their shirtsleeves on the front porches and Queens in bungalow aprons and boudoir caps tying up rose vines in the gardens. And their kingdoms in spite of the dust from the highway seemed pleasant, comfortable places to rule over.

We had two flat tires and Warren's sunbonnet blew away. It wasn't pretty country, most of it, and it must have been very hot and dirty, but nobody ever had a happier, sillier, more carefree drive than we had. Even when Warren picked a hole in the hardboiled egg I gave him to play with, from the lunch basket, and ate half of it before I noticed him, I couldn't worry about it.

We reached Moorehead City after seven o'clock.
(76)

The Maurices and the Birds were there ahead of us, but they had waited dinner.

Warren drank his milk in a daze and hardly waked up when I undressed him and slipped him into bed.

The little hotel had spread itself in our honor. They had shrimps, and oysters, and two kinds of fish, and muffins, and biscuits, and home-cured ham, and when we were sure we couldn't hold another thing, the most delectable blueberry tarts.

Clem and I walked down to the pier to look at the water after supper. Across the harbor we could see the flickering lights of Beaufort, and the barrier island where we would go for surf bathing.

We had engaged a fisherman for the next day to take us over to the islands where the Banks ponies are. I had learned to ride on one of these ponies when I was a little girl, and Clem's great uncle had brought a mare up to Vermont long ago, and Clem had ridden her descendants.

These little half-wild ponies will swim as far as eight miles from island to island, and the mares, they say, are canny enough always to keep the foals on the landward side to keep them from being washed out to sea by the tide. Once a year, the owners round them up and brand them.

We planned to fish, too, and to take Warren crabbing.

(77)

We strolled back to the hotel, through the little village, hand in hand. How salt the air smelled! There was no dust. The people we passed spoke in soft, low voices. They sounded so plaintive and gentle, and the accent was so thick, we could hardly understand what they said. As far as a hundred miles from the coast we had seen at a distance tall, gorgeously brilliant, yellow swamp lilies, and Warren had held out his hands for them. We passed some in a little shop. I thought I'd bring Warren down in the morning to see them close.

I haven't seen any more of Moorehead City, nor of the North Carolina coast than I have written here. Nor do I think I ever want to go back. No place could be so charmingly unspoilt and fresh and clean and beautiful as I remember it. There was a telegram waiting for us when we got back to the hotel, and we started home at sun-up.

Sanders, our farmer, had been hurt in an automobile accident and was dying.

9

Sanders was the only man I ever knew for certain that loved and trusted God. When Sanders spoke of God, his round face lit up with the same enthusiasm that flashes across a high school boy's when he speaks of the football captain, or I have seen the same look on a young second lieutenant's face when he tried to say what he thought of the "Old Man."

Every Sunday morning Sanders shaved and dressed up in his shiny blue suit and went to church. The suit was one of those please-don't-rain suits from the mail order catalogues. It had had the misfortune to have been thoroughly wet at some time and had shrunk tight across the back and very short in the sleeves. His hands protruded, long and awkward, for, while he wore a celluloid collar, there were no cuffs in evidence. His hands really were not awkward at all; they were cunning hands. They could tease a bolt to perform a duty it was never meant to do and magically produce motion from a gasoline engine that Clem and the garage mechanic thought needed a new part from Charlotte at the least.

His round face shone with soap and water and love for his Maker on Sunday mornings, but he carried his religion with him during the week. His was a tolerant, kindly faith with a slightly humorous quirk to it. God was a sort of benevolent landlord, and Sanders was his tenant. God's ways were mysterious. He had His own ways of doing things and was given to whims, even as earthly landlords are. Sanders was genuinely grateful to him for all the blessings of this world — and he was the one person I ever knew who I thought was, although I have known several clergymen and I went for three years to a church school.

He was in no sense bigoted. He was passionately loyal to God, himself, but he was not above apologizing for him to other people on occasion. After a hailstorm the first summer, which hit among the orchards here and there without apparent rhyme or reason, Clem commented in a somewhat ironic vein on the marvelous ways of Providence.

" Mist' Ripley," said Sanders, " God don't hardly ever aim to hit a man." But when Clem couldn't resist the inevitable, " He must be a pretty poor shot," Sanders laughed as hard an anybody.

(80)

Just the same, Clem's levity on religious matters worried Sanders a good deal. I'm sure he prayed for us.

He always felt it his responsibility to look out for us. Sanders was a shrewd trader, and while I doubt if he used his shrewdness much to help himself, he felt it his duty to use it for us.

There was Noah MacAn and the cow and the mules. Noah sold us a cow from Raphael's dairy herd. Whether he knew it or not, I am not entirely sure, but although she was a pretty thing, when the time came to breed her we found she couldn't breed, and she went dry. Sanders was genuinely distressed. There was nothing we could do about the cow, but not long afterward Noah, acting for Raphael, became interested in our pair of mules. They were fine, big mules, Samson and Goliath, without blemish except that Goliath, the off mule, had a bunch about the size of an acorn just behind his foreleg. Noah looked them over and asked, " Do you warrant them sound? " And Sanders said, " Yes, I reckon I'd call 'em sound, except o' course you see that there little bunch behind Goliath's foreleg." Noah took a look at it and felt it, and then he asked the obvious question: " Has it grown since you had him? " " It grown? " asked Sanders innocently. " Been just like you see it for the las' two months." Sanders' reputation for truth-telling was a byword and Noah traded for the mules. Sanders had told him the literal truth. What

(81)

he hadn't told him (and what Noah hadn't asked) was that Goliath hadn't been worked in the last two months. Before that, after a couple of days in the plow, the lump would swell as big as your fist.

"Miz Ripley," Sanders said, when I had qualms of conscience, "you got no call to fret about that. I was a-studyin' 'bout yore cow all the time."

One Sunday morning Sanders rattled by our house, his wife and kids piled helter-skelter in his disreputable car on their way to church. Clem and I were working in that little piece of field between the orchard and the house which we were pleased to call our front garden. A dirt terrace separated it from the orchard and kept some of the sand from blowing into the house, and we were planting honeysuckle roots in it to keep it from washing away in the terrific rains we sometimes had.

I had straightened up something like half an hour after the Sanderses had passed, to ease my back and have a refreshing look at the blue sky, which is very close to earth in the Sandhills, when I saw over the roof of our house a gigantic black cloud of smoke.

"Forest fire!" was my first, alarming thought. We had plenty of them in the late winter — people burning a ring of woods to kill boll-weevils or peach pests and carelessly (or purposely, since the more woods burned, the more pests killed is the theory) letting the fire get away.

I dropped my trowel and called to Clem to come on as I began to run towards the smoke. Once around the house I saw what it was — the Sanders' house was ablaze.

I have a bad habit of always expecting the worst, and as I ran I tried to reconstruct a mental picture of that rattle-trap car and to remember how many young Sanderses went with their parents to church. Could Mrs. Sanders have left the baby sleeping at home? She sometimes did.

Two country women and a man were standing in the roadway, staring apathetically at the blaze. One of the women called out to us as we came up — " We'd have saved somethin', Mist' Ripley, only the doors was locked."

" Good Lord! Why didn't you break them in? "

" We didn't like to."

Clem was on the porch by that time, and I was panting behind. He drove his shoulder against the door and the flimsy lock gave at once. We dragged out the sewing machine — a few chairs — some odds and ends of bedding, before the roof began to give and we had to run out to safety. My silver-mounted saddle that Clem's regiment gave me as a wedding present was stored in the back part of the house, and Clem's saddle, and my best linen, and the baby pins and trinkets I had saved from a little girl. But I didn't give them a thought at

(83)

the time. There was no child trapped in the house, no living thing.

But the pitiful possessions that Sanders and his wife had stored up as squirrels store nuts for the winter were all gone — all except the sewing machine and a few odds and ends.

I didn't have any time to worry about it, though, for a wind had sprung up and the lightwood shingles were burning with a terrific heat. Clem, with a crowd of men who had sprung up from nowhere, was moving melon crates from a shed across the road. Already sparks from the burning house were flying across and landing on the shingle roof of the shed. I don't know just when he arrived, but Sanders was on top of the roof, beating out the sparks. A boy was scooping up handfuls of sand and reaching it up to him to throw on the tiny blazes.

There was nothing I could do. It was just a matter of time — if they could keep the roof from catching long enough to move out the crates. I went in search of Mrs. Sanders. She sat on the sand, dry-eyed, with her children and the neighbor women about her.

I said what I could to comfort her. After a while, she said, " I dunno how come it to happen. All the way comin', after we first seen the smoke an' thought it might be over our way, Archie kep' sayin', ' if it should come to be our house, I hope Mist' Ripley gets his sad-

(84)

dles. They're valuable.' . . . Archie, he put 'em there jus' las' Tuesday when he oiled 'em."

There wasn't anything for me to say. I still had beds to sleep in and clothes to wear, and dishes to eat off of.

Mrs. Sanders said, " I wish't they'd saved my cloths. Babies ought to have clean cloths."

I got to know the Sanderses pretty well after the fire. I let my colored couple go and the Sanderses lived in their cabin while their new house was building. Of necessity, I did my own cooking those six weeks, and Mrs. Sanders shared my kitchen. Her cooking was of the simplest. Twice a week she baked a batch of sweet potatoes and a batch of corn bread, and the family lived on that until it was gone.

She took very little interest in the building of the new house. Sanders' chief interest seemed to be in how cheaply it could be done and how much money he could save us. Completed, it had five rooms and cost a little over five hundred dollars. We collected a thousand dollars insurance, so we really made money on the fire.

The honeydews and dewberries, out of which Sanders was to get ten percent, barely paid expenses. He kept cheerful and hopeful, though, and tied up the farm machinery with baling wire and tinkered with his twenty-eighth car. Trading cars was his recreation. He traded cars much as countrymen a generation ago used to trade horses.

It was several months after the house burned and Sanders and his family were on their way to church again. I didn't see Sanders that morning, but I know how he must have looked, his round, happy face shaved for Sunday, his square, rather well-made shoulders in his please-don't-rain suit. He was driving his latest car, a car with a seat in front and a truck body in the back. He occupied the seat alone as Mrs. Sanders was sitting in the back to keep the children from falling out.

I don't suppose they had a horn and there is little doubt in my mind that Sanders was at fault in the accident. At any rate, as they drove out past the last of Raphael's peach trees, which hid them from anyone driving down the highway, they collided broadside with a salesman from Greensboro in a new sedan.

The salesman was jarred, but not seriously hurt. The Sanders children, and Mrs. Sanders, still clinging to the baby, were strewn like bundles of rags across the highway, but they straightened up and found they were only bruised and shaken up a little.

But Sanders, who had been moved just from the driver's seat to the one beside it, lay still. His neck was broken, and though he groaned all through the night, he never regained consciousness, and at about sunrise he died.

It was the telegram telling of his accident that brought Clem and me back from the coast in such a hurry. He had been dead a whole day when we reached Samarcand.

They buried him from his father's. I didn't want to go to the funeral, but I knew I had to. We turned off the highway, drove down a long, wooded hill, and came suddenly upon a cotton field with a sun-scarred, unpainted house standing on stilts in the middle of it. About twenty cars were parked in the little yard before the porch. People were shuffling about, whispering to each other. Most of them stopped and stared at us as we got out of the car. It took me a minute to recognize those I knew in their Sunday clothes — the men, ill at ease in their badly fitting dark suits, the women in their dark or white dresses, with puzzled, quiet children clinging to their skirts.

A tall, stooped old woman came out to meet us and the crowd gave back a step as she passed through. " It's Mist' Ripley, ain't it? " she said. " I'm his mother."

All I could think to say was, " I'm sorry it had to happen."

The tears rolled down her wrinkled cheeks. " I was glad to see him die, though, an' have that terrible moanin' stop. The doctors said, him from Greensboro and Doct' Harris, too, that it didn't hurt him none. But I — I dunno. . . . His neck was broke," she added. " I'm glad the moanin' stopped."

It came to me, " Why, she feels just as I would feel! "

It surprised me that she hadn't hoped against hope, that with the literal faith of her son and daughter-in-law she hadn't prayed that the laws of nature be changed to fit her case. We understood each other. It's useless to resist the inevitable.

She jerked her head towards the house. " She's been a-prayin' all night. But — I dunno — don't seem like it's much use."

I followed her to the front room where Mrs. Sanders lay. Mrs. Sanders looked somehow younger and in-finitely pathetic in her long-sleeved high-necked cotton nightgown, with her hair plaited down in two long, thin plaits on either side of her face.

I sat down and took her hands. I said, thinking it would please her and because I didn't know what else to say, " God's will be done."

She said, in a small, dull voice, " I — I reckon so. . . . You knew him. We was on our way to church."

" Mrs. Sanders," I said, " you can stay on the farm as long as you want to. The house Archie built is as much yours as it is ours."

She looked at me as though she didn't understand me, or it didn't matter anyway.

I repeated the futile, " I wish I could help you."

" He's gone," was all she said.

" I tip-toed through the hall, passed the coffin with-out looking in, and stood with Clem in the yard. Clem pointed out Sanders' uncle, who was a champion fiddler and a moonshiner. He was a bony, sullen-looking man, as different as possible from Sanders. The two boys with him, Clem said, were Sanders' cousins and were in the moonshining business, too.

A car drove up and a large, soft-looking person with a pasty white face got out. He was treated with even more deference by the crowd than we had been. It was the preacher.

They put a glass of water on the table on the porch before him, and he took out his Bible and offered up a prayer.

It was mostly a description of the accident to the Almighty. He explained to God in a high whine that he was praying from the porch so that the stricken widow could hear him from her bed.

He finished the prayer and began to preach. . . . " And, Brethren! Think o' the pore widow, lyin' on her bed, stricken down. Think o' the five little children fatherless through life. Nobody to turn to — nowheres to go. But God needed sweet singers in his choir, an' He took Brother Sanders to sing in Heaven for Him. . . ."

I thought of Sanders' God, the kindly Father.

". . . And there sit his wicked kinfolks. . . . Maybe God took Brother Sanders away to be a lesson to them — to turn them from their wicked ways. . . ."

(89)

There was more and more. I thought it would never end. But after a while it droned off into nothingness. It was a relief when half a dozen men brought out the coffin at last, shouldered it on to a truck, and laid a patchwork quilt over it.

We walked behind it to the little, weed-grown grave-yard behind the cotton field. There were no flowers — only a wilted bunch or two of zinnias someone had brought from a late garden. In the Sandhills, the sun burns up flowers in September.

At the graveside came a ceremony I would have avoided if I could. While the mourners sang " Shall we gather at the river? " their voices weak and lifeless in the hot afternoon, they lifted back the coffin lid and one by one the whole gathering filed past. I wanted to shut my eyes, but I couldn't.

Sanders lay there in the hot sun. His honest, humorous face still held a simple dignity. They had dressed him in evening clothes. His hands, ungloved, lay folded. I couldn't take my eyes from those hands — the little cuts and bruises, the broken finger nails, all made by work for us on our farm.

10

After Sanders' death we had to find a new farmer. Old Man Britt, who lived half a mile away in the clay, had been looking after the stock since the accident. We debated engaging him permanently but hesitated to do so on account of his two bad boys, Clyde and Rob. The children had no mother and had been let run loose. We suspected them of having broken into our house once when we were away for the day, and of making off with odds and ends of tools when they had worked for us on occasion in the orchard. Neighborhood sentiment was strong against them. We decided not to engage Old Man Britt.

David Ballard was a good man. He was Mrs. Sanders' cousin and had share-cropped a farm near us. Dave had a wife and six children. The season before, his share-crop of cotton and tobacco had only paid him about two hundred and fifty dollars. On the side he had done a little moonshining to help eke out a living. Clem had patronized him until a friend of ours who patriotically served as a deputy found his still and unwittingly killed two birds with one stone by getting Dave put on probation and Clem appointed his probation officer.

We had a great deal of sympathy for Dave. Since the discovery of his still he had been working even harder than usual in the hopeless rut of his share-crops. Clem offered him the job of being our farmer. But Dave, only a few days before, had had a piece of dazzling good fortune. A grower in Pinehurst had promised him nearly twice what we could pay.

"But Mr. Ripley," he said, "There's my brother Rory. He's a good boy. You an' him might could trade."

Rory was pretty young, only twenty. But we considered that if Mrs. Sanders should want to stay on it would be better all around to have her cousin than a stranger. We sent for Rory and he and Janie, his wife, moved over.

Just before Sanders' death we had completed a two-room shack beyond the barn with the idea of putting in a family of negro tenants. It was still unoccupied. Rory and Mrs. Sanders arranged things to suit themselves and Mrs. Sanders and the children moved down to the shack. Sanders, always more intelligent than the average Sandhiller, had left her two thousand dollars life insurance.

I tried to think of some way to help Mrs. Sanders make a living for herself and the children. I had several somewhat impractical plans. The immediate one was a tide-over for the present.

It was the season for scuppernong grapes. There was an old arbor on the farm which bore heavily. One Saturday morning I drove Mrs. Sanders over to the county-seat to see the state agent demonstrate the various ways the grapes could be used. I intended to make wine out of the juice for our use, but I planned to pay Mrs. Sanders and the children for gathering them, and to give Mrs. Sanders the pulp and skins to make into jams and jellies which she could sell at the Woman's Exchange.

The demonstrator cooked and lectured all morning. She taught us besides simple jellies, how to make conserves and preserves and grape paste. I industriously took notes and peeped into the simmering pots. Mrs. Sanders sat quietly with her hands folded in her lap.

On the drive home I talked about my plans for her. She listened in apathetic silence. When I finished she said nothing. But a moment later she made an illuminating remark.

" I'm figurin'," she said, " on buildin' me a nice house over next my mother's. I always kind o'hankered to live there . . . Archie " she added, tears and pride mingled in her voice, " done well by us."

Poor Mrs. Sanders! Two thousand dollars all in a lump seemed to her unlimited riches.

Earnestly I pointed out the advantages of five percent bonds. She was a gentle soul. She tried to show an interest in what I was saying. But I realized the futility of going on when she said, palpably to please me, " I'm mighty glad I seed that woman make the jelly, though. I reckon me an' the children would enjoy it fine ourselves this winter."

Everyone wants to run his life his own way. Mrs. Sanders was " in the notion " to build a house. She stayed with us several months longer and they moved over to her mother's and built it. Naturally it was a great relief to us, and I think it has worked out not too badly for her. At any rate the last time I saw her and the children they all looked well.

It was fortunate for us that winter was coming and the farm work was slackening. Clem, with Rory and Old Man Britt, harvested the corn and pea-vine hay. Rory did the fall plowing in the orchard and we laid the little trees by for the winter.

From the start we found that there was a great difference between farming with Rory and farming with Sanders. Rory was a chinless, rabbit-like individual, who had to be told each day what to do, and usually how to do it. We were used to Sanders tactfully suggesting, "Cap'n Ripley, if it's clear tomorrow I aim to sow them beans," and adding as a sop to the owner's authority, "that is, if you ain't got nothin' else that's pushin'."

Rory took no responsibility. He did what he was told and no more. Sanders had been painstaking with the stock, but Rory even had to be told to change the horses' bedding. Old Man Britt was a clay dweller, with a somber contempt for anything bred in the sand. Rory's slowness kept him in a constant state of fury. He never came out directly with it, but there were continual mutterings about "that dam' Sandhiller, draggin' his differential 'round this place."

In late October the migration south starts. We were excited and glad to see our friends back again. They all seemed new and strange in their city clothes when they first came down. It's a phenomenon that happens every year. For a little there's a hum of talk — New York and the plays, Southampton, Murray Bay, somebody's dinner at the Colony Club. And then, gradually, these things are forgotten and the talk swings about to peaches and Pinehurst gossip and the Harvest Ball, and it's all as though they had never been away.

There were dinners and parties, and for the time being Clem and I even forgot our money troubles. Except for Rory's wages and a little to Old Man Britt, not much was going out on the farm this time of year. When we

(95)

added up the figures at the end of October we congratulated ourselves on what a cheap month it had been. Although we expected to get in extra labor for the pruning next month, now the trees were bigger, I somehow couldn't quite make myself believe that we were going to run into very much expense.

I felt encouraged. The heat had broken. It was fun to take walks in the woods now the red-bugs were gone. It was fun to slip and slide through the sand of the orchard now that it was cooler. It was more than fun, it was the breath of life, to drive over to Pinehurst and listen to people talk who didn't double their negatives. Clem was at work on another story. This time it was about a hard-boiled Marine who fell heir to a kingdom in Mongolia. We were sure it only had to be finished and mailed to be money in the bank.

We had traded the mules for a pair of Morgan horses. They were bred on the Samarcand plantation from a beautiful sire, Tammerlane. Sand land is light, and although they had been in the plow Clem and I thought they might work out passably under saddle. I'd put on my riding clothes those warm fall mornings and we'd go down to the barn, catch the horses in the paddock, and curry and groom them before we saddled up. Then we'd ride down the wood roads or over to Samarcand for the mail.

Fanny, the mare, was a pretty enough creature. The

gelding was heavier and clumsy. His gallop was like a ship on a rough sea. Fanny had been smoothly gaited at one time but the farm work had ruined her gaits and hardened her mouth. She pulled constantly. She generally took the bit in her teeth and ran when she was headed homeward, the gelding, with Clem urging him along, pounding behind. There was a quality of strain strong in sensitive Fanny after long days in the plow. A nervous energy carried her on, but she was apt to stumble and fall to her knees even on the smooth sand road. I rode her on a snaffle bit after I realized that the curb didn't help to control her but only aggravated her nervousness. But the snaffle didn't help either.

Clem and I each realized separately, long before we admitted it to each other, that you can't have it both ways. Using horses to plow with pretty well ruins them for pleasure riding. We never actually spoke of it, but gradually one excuse or another served to keep us from going to the barn in the morning, and after a while we stopped riding altogether.

Even so, the turning of the leaves along the road had been a pleasant thing to see and there had been a clean fragrance in the October wind that panted for winter to come.

November came and we began the pruning. The trees were bigger and the work was heavier than last year — and then, too, Rory was not nearly so good as

(97)

Sanders had been. We engaged Old Man Britt and his boy, Clyde, to help. Extra men, extra saws, extra pruning shears — the French model, which cost more on account of the duty. (No American manufacturer, under a system of Protection, would bother to put out a decent set of pruning shears for a farmer to use.)

We were going to be sure of having the work done efficiently and in plenty of time. Any reader of farm journals knows the value of being forehanded. Clem studied the government bulletins for the most approved methods of pruning and put them into effect. By Christmas our orchard was beautifully pruned and had also been sprayed with dormant spray. All the brush had been hauled away (a gang of darky girls had been hired for this) and stacked neatly to dry for burning. Our orchard was clean as a whistle.

This gave us two months leeway before the spring cultivating had to be done. We were delighted with our orchard and ourselves. When we drove down the highway past orchards still unpruned, we glowed with pride. Notably orchards belonging to native Sandhillers were latest in being pruned. In some of these only one or two men worked and half of the trees were still untouched. " Shiftless! " said I with the satisfaction of superiority.

But not for long.

We totted up the books for December. The extra labor figured up to a bigger total than we had realized.

Then, about two o'clock one morning Clem waked me up to ask me a question. "Katti," he said, "I hadn't thought, had you, what's Rory going to do with his time these next two months?"

I hadn't thought either, but my pride in the clean orchard collapsed like a pricked soufflé. Clem and Rory alone could have pruned and sprayed the two-year-old trees in four months just as well as four men had in two — and Rory was working by the month. That was a simple fact that hadn't occurred to either of us before.

There should have been that year, just as there has always been since then, a frenzied spring week when the brush isn't yet hauled out of the orchard and the dormant spray not on, though the buds are ready to burst. The ideal is to have the winter work just finished in time to begin the spring work, of course. But if you can't be exact (and on a farm when you have to cope with inexactness of weather, how can you be?) it's better to be pushed in the spring. If you absolutely have to have extra labor you can go out and hire it then. But more often than not, you can manage without it. How we missed Sanders!

Since then I have observed a good many farms, and it seems to me the farmers who get along best are usually the ones whose farm machinery is tied up with baling wire and whose fences are unpainted. Undermanned, and with cheap, frequently second-hand, tools, these farms are economically run. The overhead is kept down and there is a chance for a profit. Time-saving devices on a farm are a costly economy. Time is one thing a farmer (who works a twelve to fourteen hour day) has plenty of.

Being up to date and forehanded on a farm is an expensive luxury. It was our good fortune to learn this lesson early and cheaply.

It's a temptation to have everything shipshape and use lots of white paint, but farms will seldom support very much spit-and-polish. When you see a farm with fences and barns beautifully painted, with gates swinging on well-oiled hinges, with milking machines and smooth-running tractors, it is usually costing some wealthy business man from the city a lot of money.

11

―――――――――――

It was the night of January sixth ('22) — Old Christmas night. (For many of the older Sandhills people the Julian Calendar still exists, and the days between Old and New Christmas are kept as a holiday season.) I remember because we had difficulty getting a man to help Rory cut and haul wood in the interval and we had rationed out what we had to last until January seventh.

There was a dance that night. It might have been one of the Boyds' dances. They generally gave one that time of year. It might have been just a party of us going to dance at one of the hotels. It's a funny thing, when I remember the rest of the night so vividly, that I can't remember anything about that dance.

We went over to Pinehurst early in the afternoon. Warren was digging with a spoon in the sand in front of our house. He had on a pale blue coat and beret. His cheeks were red and rounded like winter apples. Sarah, our present cook, was improving the shining hour, since she knew I would see her, by sweeping the brick walk. Warren threw down his spoon and began to tug at the broom. " Baby do dat! baby feep! ' Everything seemed normal and usual as we drove away.

I don't know what time the rain began but it was midnight when we drove home and it had been raining some time then. A bitter cold wind had sprung up. Our little house was a blur except where the pale lamplight shone from the windows of Warren's room. Clem stopped the car and I jumped out and ran through the wet to the side door while he drove down to the shed. I let myself in.

When I came to Warren's room I saw old Sarah fast asleep in a chair before the embers of the fire, her head buried in her arms. Lacy, the ten-year-old boy who helped her, lay curled on the rug at her feet asleep, too. There was nothing remarkable in that, but as I tiptoed past the crib to waken Sarah I peeped in at the baby.

Warren's eyes were wide open and they had rolled back in their sockets until only the whites and the rim of the iris showed.

They snapped back into place suddenly, as a doll's do, when I stooped to touch him. He pushed me away with his hands. . . . " Go 'way, bad boys! Baby not do dat no mo'." I didn't have to touch his forehead

(102)

with my lips to know that he was feverish, but I had found the clinical thermometer and learned that he had a temperature of a hundred and five before Clem came in.

I had shaken old Sarah awake and she stood blinking her eyes like a sleepy owl. . . . " Po' li'l baby — po' li'l baby! " she kept saying. I told her to pack Warren's clothes while Lacy heated me some water to give the child a sponge bath. Clem was stoically ringing the telephone. He knew and I knew that the chances of getting a call through to Pinehurst at that hour were practically nil. Even if he could raise Mrs. Morgan there was always the Central at West End who had to connect us and she didn't live at her exchange. The 'phone was quite dead. We learned later that the storm had blown a tree across the wire.

There was no hospital at Pinehurst or Southern Pines at this time. I was afraid the hotels mightn't take a sick child in. The only local doctor I knew of then lived miles away, back somewhere over in the clay, and was a sort of " yarb " doctor. I didn't even consider him. Raleigh and Greensboro, where there were good hospitals, were each between eighty and a hundred miles from us. Columbia was farther — a hundred and fifty miles — but in Columbia was the best baby specialist I have ever known and Warren had been his patient once before.

(103)

My family lived in Columbia, too, and we had to consider the expense of a hotel for ourselves for a length of time as against visiting. I knew Warren was pretty sick, but I wasn't panicky — not that time — and it seemed to me that the difference between driving a hundred miles and a hundred and fifty was negligible.

Clem was for waiting until morning, but I wouldn't wait. Sarah grumbled, "You'll kill the chile, tekin' him out'n his warm baid on such a night," but I knew that a young child's illness may become acute in a few hours — sometimes it's now or never.

Clem filled the car with gasoline and oil and water. We had traded in the Ford for a Chevrolet touring car. The curtains were already up. Warren hardly stirred when I wrapped him in my overcoat. Lacy was whimpering and old Sarah looked as if she might burst into tears.

Old Sarah, all two hundred and twenty pounds of black kindness and devotion to Warren, dropped me the funny little half-curtsey she'd been taught back in Virginia, and said, her voice quavering, "You write an' tell me, please ma'm, how my baby boy gits on. I cain't read, but Lacy kin right smart."

It flashed through my mind, "Sarah always has taken more trouble to amuse Warren and play with him than I ever did. It hasn't been two days since Clem saw the big old fat mountain running around on all

(104)

fours in the kitchen barking like a dog, while Warren screamed with delight."

We didn't have an umbrella, but Sarah followed me out in the rain, with a blanket held over the baby and me. The world must be a good place to have people in it like old Sarah. When I think of how much of herself she gave me, including gratitude, for a little house to sleep in, three pretty skimpy meals a day, and five dollars cash a week, I feel small and ashamed.

We were warm and comfortable inside the car in our heavy coats. Warren snuggled down into the crook of my arm and dropped off into a fitful doze.

I said to Clem, " Think of living in this marvelous twentieth century, when you can shut yourself up in a little steel box and shoot yourself a hundred and fifty miles in five hours."

Clem said, " With luck you might."

I thought of women fifty years ago, hovering all night over a sick child, trying first one thing and then another, going it blind. Something Sanders once said brought me up with a sudden jerk — " You cain't expect to raise 'em all. You' bound to lose one or two." I held Warren tighter. I felt awed at my own good fortune.

I said, " Clem, do you realize that we belong to the chosen few in this world? Why do you suppose we were given a so much better chance to take care of ourselves and Warren than most people are? "

(105)

Clem kept his eyes on the road. The rain streamed in black lines across the windshield. He said, " I can tell better about that when we get to Columbia."

The Chevrolet slithered from side to side of the slick clay road, and Warren slept on and the miles piled up behind us. There aren't many villages on that road and those we passed were dark this time of night. The country looked as though Arthur Rackham might have drawn it. The leafless trees were twisted into grotesque shapes. Occasional cabins, outlined by the headlights, squatted like big toads in the mud. Witches should have ridden broomsticks through the wind and the streamers of rain. Warren waked and moaned and slept again.

The road was possible, considering the weather, until we passed Camden. We had made good time. We should be in Columbia in a little over an hour.

A few miles farther on the rain, which had been slackening for the last half hour or more, stopped. The good road stopped, too.

Before us, out of the black night, rose a white barricade. Clem jammed on his brakes and got out to read the home-made sign. The second the motion of the car stopped, Warren began to scream in obvious terror. He struggled and fought and seemed not to know the sound of my voice.

Clem yelled above the din, " It says, ' Highway

(106)

under repair. Advise taking Perseval Road to Columbia.' Do you know where that is? ''

"No," I called back. " How should I? "

" Well, it's a cinch I don't," said Clem. " There are no more directions — no arrow — nothing."

A cross-road, hardly more than a wheel track, the furrows ploughed deep in mud, cut across at right angles to the road we were on. We could take our choice of direction.

Clem got back into the car and started the engine. The vibration and noise soothed Warren and he quieted and snuggled back into my arms. At random, we chose the right fork.

Once, long ago, we had driven through a little town in Ohio. We asked a man on the sidewalk the way to the post office.

" Post office? " he said. " Why sure — you just drive down to Paint Street and turn to your left and — "

" But where," Clem interrupted him, "is Paint Street? "

" Paint Street? " the man repeated. " Paint Street? Why you don't know where Paint Street is? " He just couldn't conceive of anyone not knowing where Paint Street was.

I suppose whoever tacked up that sign thought every-one would know the Perseval Road. . . . The *Perse-*

val Road? Sure, everyone *must* know the Perseval Road.
. . . I found I was laughing hysterically.

Clem had the car in low and we crept through the
mud, our back wheels spinning for horrible eon-long
seconds in the deep puddles. The road wound on endlessly. There were no houses — there was nothing but
road and woods and empty fields.

" Would anyone have named a road like this such
an imposing name? " I wondered doubtfully.

Clem said, " We can't go back — there's no place
to turn. We have to go on."

We stuck in a deep mudhole. The left hind wheel
spun and dug deeper into the mud. Clem got out and
jacked it up and filled the hole in with brush. Warren's head felt cooler to my lips, now the fever was
dropping with the passing night. His crying was a thin
wail, like a cat's, seeming to come from far off. I
propped him up on the seat with his head resting against
my arm while I took the wheel and Clem pushed from
behind and I steered the car to firmer ground.

My right arm which had held the weight of Warren's head for hours, had been numb and dead. But
when I took the wheel the circulation came back with
an agonizing stinging. Surely this road must lead
somewhere.

It couldn't have been many minutes when we struck
the highway. To our left was a barricade with a sign,

(108)

"Detour to Camden," so it must have been the Perseval Road we were on.

To our right was a sign, "Fifteen miles to Columbia," . . . "And good roads," I said to Clem. "We'll be home in half an hour now."

Clem was driving as fast as he dared on the slick road. I leaned back and tried to relax. "We've done it!" I thought. "We're practically home — it's all over but the shouting. I can pass the responsibility to the doctor; he'll give Warren something and have him well in a jiffy. I can go to bed and sleep and rest my arm."

We passed a shed, crossed a railroad track, passed a one-story building, probably a store, saw a light from the window of a house ahead, heard the choke and sputter of our motor, and glided smoothly to a full stop before the door of the first lighted house we had passed for an hour.

We both knew what it was. Those long miles, pulling through the mud in low, had used quantities of gasoline. We were out of gas.

"God, what a piece of luck!" Clem's voice held a sort of awe. "To have it happen here instead of back there in the woods!"

The door of the house was within a few feet of us. Clem pounded on it. I could see shadows of people passing before the windows. Though the blinds were

(109)

closed there were cracks that the light shone through. I could hear men's voices and the shrill, excited laughter of women.

Clem hammered at the door again. . . . " Hello! " he called. " Can you tell me where I can get some gas? "

Somebody slid back a bolt, cautiously. The door opened a crack. Whoever it was evidently got a good view of Clem. I heard a boyish voice say, " Naw, it ain't nobody — that is, it ain't the sheriff. Jus' some so-an'-so outa gas or sup'm." The door banged shut.

Clem kicked it. The bolt slid back again. This time the door flew wide open. A tall white man, old and haggard, reeled against the light. In the crook of his arm, the two half supporting each other, leaned a slender mulatto girl. A half grown white boy and several negro men and women stood behind them.

" Get off my porch! " stormed the man. " What you mean, kicking at my door in the dead of night? You ain't go not business here, you — "

I was afraid of what might happen. The door had hardly opened before I was out of the car and standing with Warren in my arms on the running board.

The old man caught sight of me. The cursing broke off suddenly in his thoat. He pushed the negro girl behind him — staggered — tried to bow — staggered straight again.

" I beg yo' pardon, ma'm. I didn't know the' was a

(110)

lady here. If the's anything I can do, it'll be a pleasure, ma'm."

In spite of his surroundings, he achieved a sort of dignity.

" Thank you, sir," I said. " I have a sick child and we're trying to get him to Columbia. Could you let us have a few gallons of gasoline? "

" Cert'nly, ma'm." . . . He went on, thickly, " Anything to oblige a lady."

There was something about him — long ago the country squire had ridden over, resplendent in a high collar, to pay his respects to another squire's daughter.

He turned to the white boy. . . " Sam, you git the gentleman the gas." He waved his hand towards the dark beyond the house. " Sir, Sam will git you the gasoline."

But Sam demurred. " I'm skeered," he objected, " to go so fur in the dark by myself."

Clem said, " Run and get a kerosene can or a bucket and I'll go with you. You just show me the way."

It wasn't until they disappeared in the shadows that I began to feel alarmed. The negro men, sullen and silent, had all drifted away. Only the old man, the mulatto girl, and another woman stood in the hallway.

The old man asked me to come in the house. " Rest yo'self and warm yo'self before the fire, ma'm," he said.

(111)

" Thank you," I said. " But they won't be gone long and as soon as my husband comes back we must be on our way."

" You taking yo' chap to the doctor? " he asked. " I'm a sort of doctor. Lemme take a look at him."

" Oh, no thank you," I said quickly. I could hear Warren's quick breathing. He was asleep again. I shrank back in the corner of the car, lest that lewd old creature come closer to him or to me.

My refusal, my evident distaste, made him angry. " You don't believe me, eh? You don't believe I'm a doctor? "

He was standing by the running board, peering in at me. The mulatto girl was by his side. They filled the car with the reek of cheap whiskey.

" I'm sure you're a fine doctor," I told him. " But I'm taking my little boy to a specialist in Columbia. A baby doctor — a doctor who just treats babies."

" You are, eh? What's wrong with the chap? "

" A bad cold, I think."

" You do? " he said. " You do? . . . Well, have you thought of diphtheria? Have you thought of kidney trouble? Have you thought of smallpox? Have you thought of tooberculosus?" His voice had risen. His trembling hands gripped the side of the car and the little Chevrolet shook beneath them.

I bit my lip to keep from crying. I was so tired. "Don't trouble to stay here with me," I said as calmly and soothingly as I could. "You are very kind, but we are quite all right."

"Lizzie!" the tone of his voice changed suddenly to a sharp command. "If the lady's too good to associate with us, we'll retire in good order to the house."

This time he made me a very good bow. "Good evenin', ma'm."

It was many minutes before Clem came back with the gas. They had had to go half a mile to a farm back in the woods. I'm afraid I did cry then — Warren and I both. The tears ran quickly down my cheeks, but Warren's cry was such a weak complaint that I was frightened out of my wits.

It was already day when we reached Columbia. The doctor found that Warren had a streptococcus infection in both ears. He hung between life and death for a few days. If we had waited until daylight to leave the farm it would have been late to puncture the ears and make them drain. Those few hours we saved gave him his chance for life.

The next week I happened to see Lizzie on Main Street in an extra coat of mine which had been on the back seat of the car. She must have slipped it out while the old man was ranting at me. I let it go. The coat wasn't worth much and I couldn't have stood the scene.

(113)

After all, they had been kind enough in their way and the gas had saved Warren's life.

That was a bad night, but it wasn't the only one. We had a similar experience when Warren had diphtheria, and there were accidents once or twice to farm people. There must be a delicate, nice adjustment to combine the twentieth century with the nineteenth until they meet in harmony.

Fortunately Warren was a strong, husky child. Certainly he got plenty of sunshine and fresh air on the farm. And yet, in the dead country, away from other children, he caught diphtheria (and there was not another case in the county), malaria (and there was practically none in the section), chicken-pox (we traced that to a child on the place who had it), and whooping cough and flu. The theory that country air is pure and free from germs doesn't go with me any more. Another time I'd take a chance on impure city air and a good doctor three blocks away to nip the illness in the bud before it has a chance really to develop.

I could never bring myself to take births and deaths as casually as do the country folk, who are psychologically our great grandfathers and grandmothers. I couldn't agree philosophically with Sanders — " You can't expect to raise 'em all." I belong to a generation that intends to raise 'em all.

(114)

12

In the Sandhills first it's winter, wind and rain and the curtains up on the car for the long drive to Pinehurst, cold, clean, sunny days and slow work pruning in the orchard, and then quite suddenly one day spring comes and the peach buds burst. Our little trees had a few blossoms this year ('23). They meant nothing, at the most a few immature little peaches that would fall off before they ripened, but just the same there was something exciting about those few deep pink blossoms. The orchard was beginning to look like an orchard rather than a toy. Even the birds were treating it seriously. A pair of cardinals began a nest in one of the little trees.

Rory was doing the spring cultivating with Fanny and the gelding in the two-horse plow. Fanny stepped high and lathered in the collar and did twice the work she should. The orchard reeked with the smell of fertilizer.

The high spring winds blew clouds of white dust into the house. On the floors were left footprints — size eights that were Clem's, queer misshapen ones with odd projections that were Sarah's, big bare feet that were Lacy's, and little bare feet that were Warren's, my own that wandered about from room to room. I was packing away blankets and rugs, sorting out letters and magazines, getting ready for the long summer.

One evening when the orchards were in full bloom the Derbys and Maurices came over to have dinner with us. It was warm and pleasant when they arrived. They had their light coats unbuttoned. We were halfway through dinner in our funny little three-cornered dining room, and Lacy was bringing in the salad plates when, with a sudden unheralded whistle of wind, one of the long French doors crashed open.

Lacy jumped to shut it. Roger Derby stopped in the middle of a sentence to stare with a worried crease between his eyes.

" Is that a north wind starting up? "

We listened. There was a whistling and moaning in the forest beyond the orchard. Windows rattled. Lacy built up the fire with lightwood, which warmed and brightened the room. But it couldn't lessen the chill which had settled over the spirits of our guests.

(116)

The Derby and Maurice orchards were in full bearing and that north wind meant no good to the peach crop.

By the time we finished dinner and went into the living room it was beginning to be quite cold. Mr. Maurice stepped outdoors to feel the temperature. The mercury was dropping fast. There was every reason to think that when the wind died down toward morning a still freeze would settle over the orchards killing the delicate blossoms.

Everyone was restless. Presently Mr. Maurice put on his overcoat and buttoned it up.

" I haven't any smudges this year," he said, " but I am going home to set the woods on fire on the north side and let this wind blow the warm air over."

Roger said, " Go ahead. I haven't put smudges out either and there aren't woods enough to burn near me, so I'll just have to luck it. I doubt if burning will do you any good but it's worth trying."

" Roger," I said, " Isn't there anything you can do? Mayn't this freeze mean the loss of your whole crop? "

" Roger! " Elizabeth Derby said, " Why haven't we smudges? "

" I doubt if they do much good, Elizabeth," he told her. " Smudges only raise the temperature about four degrees — the blossoms freeze at twenty-eight. If it drops to twenty-four the smudges won't help. If I had

(117)

had smudges I'd have burnt them night before last
when the weather was threatening so they'd be gone by
now anyway."

Smudges are piles of lightwood put at intervals
throughout the orchard. The labor of gathering and
cutting the lightwood and building the smudges and
keeping them lit comes to a good deal. Then if you burn
them because it threatens to be a cold night they're
gone. You can build others and burn every coolish night
but if a night comes just a degree colder than twenty-
four your smudges are useless, and it is just as likely to
drop to twenty-three as it is to stop at twenty-four.
Even at that time growers had found by experience that
smudges were not worth while.

I thought, " Roger Derby knows a lot about peaches.
If there was anything he could do he'd be doing it."

All night long the north wind blew. I woke in the
early morning when it died down and the icy chill
settled. I pulled up a blanket and thanked God our
peaches were not bearing yet.

As it turned out Roger had a good crop and Mr.
Maurice lost most of his. Weather hits orchards queerly.
There is very little you can do about it. The Derby trees
may have been on a little higher ground or the blossoms may have been a little less or a little further advanced and therefore in a less critical stage. It's a matter
of luck.

(118)

"But Clem," I said days afterwards, when I remembered what I had been told during our first few weeks in the section, "I thought we didn't have freezes in the Sandhills."

Clem squinted in the spring sunshine as he looked through the open window at the orchard. He frowned.

"Oh well, maybe this is our freeze for the next twenty years," he said. "It does make you feel kind of helpless though, doesn't it — like playing in a crap game against loaded dice?"

"Oh sure," I thought, "it's a fluke, this freeze. We're lucky it happened before our crop comes on."

A good many of our friends lost all or a part of their crops. But '21 had been a year of plentiful fruit in the Sandhills and high prices. Late peaches had brought as much as six dollars a crate. Also '22 had been a good year. If a grower needed money now to carry on with the banks were willing and anxious to lend on orchards. And there was the very comforting thought that the trees would benefit immensely by a year's rest, and would bear most bountifully next season. On the whole the growers accepted the freeze gracefully and cheerfully.

Far more important than the freeze, if we had known it, was a rumor that was spreading through the Sandhills. It was hardly that. It was rather, as somebody put it, " Roger Derby spreading his fool pessimism." For Roger was the Cassandra of the peach crop. Roger was talking overproduction and Roger was pointing out that '22 had not been so good a year as '21 so far as prices went. Roger was insisting on reminding people of how many new orchards had been and were being planted both here and in Georgia.

Up to now, at the season when our Sandhills crop came in, we had had the market practically to ourselves. North Georgia's acreage had been negligible. South Georgia's crop was over, and Virginia and the northern states ripened long after we did. But for the last few years the real estate agents and other boosters had been trying to create a boom in peach lands and had been planting orchards themselves to sell. Not twenty-five percent of these men were, or ever expected to be, legitimate peach growers. Most of them had no idea of ever picking a crop from the trees they planted. They planted them as a real estate speculation — for quick and profitable sale.

New orchards were being put in not only in our section but in north Georgia and in south Georgia. The county agents and newspapers in South Carolina had discovered that their state's soil was eminently suitable for peaches and were exhorting the farmers to climb up on the band wagon. Tennessee was planting large acreages. The tale of huge profits in peaches had been

(120)

widely advertised and the bees were flocking to the honey.

Not only had the acreage in the Sandhills doubled and tripled in the last few years but many of these new orchards in other sections, especially north Georgia, Roger pointed out, would come into bearing at the same season as ours and would prove direct competitors to us.

He explained patiently. "The last thing we growers want is a peach boom. We are going to be overproduced if we don't watch out. New York is the key to the market. When New York has eighty cars of peaches a day we get a whale of a price. When a hundred and twenty roll in we get a fair price, but without much margin of profit to tide us over bad years when the crops are short. When two hundred cars a day pour into New York, with the same percentage over their capacity going to other cities, the market will be flooded and the price will drop below the cost of production. It is true of all perishable crops."

But nobody paid much attention. One day he was talking to Clem about it. Half in fun he suggested that Clem write to our local newspapers a series of bone-headed letters widely exaggerating the future of peaches, which he would then answer telling the facts. They were to be a sort of straw man for Roger to knock down, and would keep the fear of overproduction in people's minds.

(121)

All through the summer Clem, his tongue in his cheek, wrote letters. They were signed Q. W. Erty, those being the first six letters on the typewriter. Roger's answers, we thought, flayed poor Mr. Erty alive, but Erty would always come back in answer to sound figures with a good old platitude about God's gift to mankind, the bountiful peaches.

Clem let himself go and entered into the spirit of the thing. Q. W. Erty became a real character. He was a hard-shelled Fundamentalist, pompous, flowery and amazingly dumb. In one way the letters had the desired effect. People became interested and began writing letters on their own.

But presently a curious situation developed. The people were all in favor of Mr. Erty. They were violently upholding his views. Here was this fine upright Mr. Erty, they said, trying to build up and boom the country, and that Roger Derby was just a plain bellyacher and knocker. More power to you, Mr. Erty!

Clem made the Erty letters even dumber than before but it was no use. People have a faculty of believing what they want to believe. All the stuff Clem made Mr. Erty say was purposely full of holes, but the real estate men who had peach lands to sell and some of the growers who already had their all in orchards, were so anxious to have it true they insisted on thinking it was. Roger's plain, common sense arguments, with their

(122)

damning array of facts and figures, were a bitter pill they refused to swallow.

The letters were a complete boomerang. Next fall when we came back from the North, where we had been with Clem's family, we found Mr. Erty was a real person in a great many people's minds. We actually knew people who had friends who were friends of Mr. Erty. They said he lived somewhere over near Vass. We even heard it suggested that he ought to run for the legislature.

I think at this time only one person took Roger very seriously. Milton Bird, who had been a good business man before he was an orchardist and who had married a girl of canny New England stock, sold his place for what he had spent on it less his own time and possible interest on the investment. The boom was still on. He could have traded it for another orchard, or unimproved peach land and a cash bonus perhaps, but he wanted all cash. It was an indication of the rotten bottom the boom had — when he wanted straight cash for his place he had to take much less than if he had been willing to trade. In time of a boom not much real money passes. It is mostly one piece of real estate swapped for another.

We were far more worried and disturbed over losing the Birds, our closest neighbors, than we were over the overproduction. At this time we couldn't believe that anything really serious could happen to the peach situa-

tion for the legitimate growers like ourselves. Possibly
to somebody else's orchard but not to ours. My eyes
followed Clem's to our own little trees, sturdy, healthy.
" Thousands shall fall at thy right hand but it shall not
come nigh thee."

13

Like the farm animals, the birds, and the rabbits, Rory and Janie had a baby in the spring.

It was part of my dream, the insistent tap, tap, tap, like the blows of a tack hammer, but there was the steady accompaniment of " Hello! Hello! Hello! " that forced me awake.

I ran across the cold floor to the window. It was a white moonlight night. I recognized Rory at the edge of the orchard in the act of stooping to pick up some sand. As I called " What's the matter, Rory? " the sand rattled against the windowpane.

" Miz Ripley, I'd like to speak to Mist' Ripley," Rory called back hoarsely. There was an excited tremor in his voice.

Two years in the Sandhills had taught me that, no matter how trifling the business, the Southern poor white will not do it with a woman, if he can possibly avoid it. I didn't stop to coax Rory. I shook Clem awake and he got up, shivering, and took my place at the window. I could hear Rory, an excited fear and pride struggling for mastery as he spoke.

"Mr. Ripley, hit's Janie. She's took. Kin I git your car and go to Tarville for the doctor, and " — now a hesitancy and doubt crept into his voice — " will you send Miz Ripley to set with her 'til I git back? "

Even as I called " All right, Rory; I'll go," I was thoroughly annoyed. This convention of a wife's being treated as a sort of appurtenance to her husband was something I had never been able to get used to.

Rory yelled, " Then that's all right, Mist' Ripley." His gawky shape disappeared on the run in the direction of the car shed.

Clem built a fire of lightwood chips for me and I stood in front of it and put on my clothes, all the time inveighing against Janie, who couldn't have a baby born in daylight. I dreaded the night before me but I didn't have any idea how full of ugly reality it was to be. Don't ever believe that husky peasant women don't suffer. And yet poor Janie, she's had three babies under very much the same conditions since.

I shivered a little, not entirely from cold, as I stepped out into the night. There was nothing Clem could do, and I couldn't see any point in his dressing to walk the short distance to Janie's with me. He had to get up

(126)

early in the morning and no doubt Rory would want the day off.

I ran the scant quarter of a mile down through the orchard. The trees stuck up black in the loose grey sand like trees in a real estate man's miniature window display. Around the cabin stood the dead stalks of Sanders' own acre of cotton. The cabin windows were brightly firelit.

Mrs. Sanders, who was Rory's cousin, opened the door for me. Ruby, her little daughter, wan and tired, clung to her skirt. Mrs. Sanders looked, as we say in North Carolina, beaten down. Even her voice held a pathetic quaver.

" I can't never bear the sight of blood since the accident," she explained to me in a whisper. " I'll go along." She held a coat in her hands. " Come on, Ruby," she said, " Miz Ripley's come. Let's we go."

" You going? " I said in amazement. " You going to leave me here alone? "

She gave a quick glance across the room. " The doctor'll come purty quick and help ye out," she told me. " We was just waitin' 'til you got here so's she wouldn't be all to herself."

I looked past the two of them to the bed where Rory's large, blonde, rather pretty girl wife lay, white and still as death, her eyes closed, the patchwork quilt pulled high about her face.

(127)

" The baby'll come any minute," whispered Mrs. Sanders. "I dunno — seems like I can't stand the sight of blood."

I could see by the trembling of Mrs. Sanders' mouth and the nervous way she rubbed her hands one over the other that she would be worse than useless. I nodded to her to go along.

" C'mon, Ruby," she said, " I left you plenty of lightwood, Miz Ripley."

Ruby Sanders said, " I'm goin' stay here and see Janie git it." Ruby was about six or seven years old.

Mrs. Sanders began to coax her. " But Ruby," she said, " t'aint right fer little girls. You c'mon with Ma."

Ruby stood her ground. " I ain't agoin' a step. I'm goin' stay and see it borned." She sat down on the floor and began to unlace her shoes.

I was poking up the fire. I saw a kettle of water had been put on to boil.

" Take her along, Mrs. Sanders," I said. " She can't stay here."

Mrs. Sanders tried wheedling but Ruby shook her little brown head and kept on undoing her shoelaces. Mrs. Sanders looked at me helplessly. " I don't know what I can do, ma'm. Seems like she won't come." She had her hand on the doorknob. " You be good now, Ruby, and mind Miz Ripley."

(128)

" But she can't stay here," I insisted.

Mrs. Sanders looked doubtfully at Ruby. " I dunno. Just seems like I can't do a thing with her."

As though the words had been a signal the girl on the bed suddenly began to scream. " Oh, God! Oh, God! Oh, God! " The little room was filled with agony and fear.

I grabbed Ruby by the shoulders and jerked her to her feet, one shoe off and one shoe on, like the nursery rhyme. " You get out of here quick," I screamed above the racket. " On your way — run! "

Ruby scuttled through the door like a scared rabbit.

Having had a baby of my own (and I was thankful then I'd had him without an anesthetic) I knew in a vague way what to expect and what Janie ought to do.

I put my hands under her shoulders and tried to pull her up. " Try to get up, Janie," I told her. " Lean on the bed and bear down."

She kept her eyes tightly shut. She seemed not to hear me. She lay rigid, only her mouth moved — screaming. She was much bigger and heavier than I. I couldn't budge her. I bathed her head with cool water — just to be doing something. After a while she stopped for breath. She asked for a drink of water.

" Please get up, Janie," I said. " The sooner it's born the better you'll feel."

(129)

"I got to scream," she whispered hoarsely. "Hit hurts me so!" she began again.

I looked about the room. The sewing machine, the other bed with its pile of patchwork quilts and sheets made of flour sacks, the alarm clock on the mantel, the two split-bottom chairs — there was no help in any of them.

"Please, Janie," I cried. "Stop, you frighten me."

She hesitated, opened her eyes. "I'm goin' to die — I'm goin' to die," she moaned.

I pulled the covers straight on the bed. "Oh, no you're not," I told her as confidently as I could.

Her face twitched as the pains came back and she began to scream again. It went on like this for a long time. A quiet interval when I begged her to get up and walk, to do anything to help herself — an endless time when that agonizing noise split the air. Part of it was involuntary. She was in pain. But part of it was convention, I knew. She was behaving as she thought she should under the circumstances. It was an opportunity to "take on" and she was taking on. From babyhood she had doubtless seen and heard births either in the same room with the lying-in woman or from the "other room." There's not much privacy in a two or three room cabin. Births and deaths are enacted, if not before the eyes of the entire family, certainly within earshot.

I got kind of used to the screaming. I put more wood on the fire. There was a big knot of lightwood with a clean, pitchy smell that lit up the whole room brilliantly and made the lamp look pale.

I was sitting by the bed holding her damp hand when a hand fell on my shoulder. I turned to greet the Tarville doctor, the man who was used to births — your wife or, at a pinch, your cow.

He was red and jovial and his breath reeked of whiskey, but, Lord, I was glad to see him.

" What's all this, girl? " he cried brusquely. There was a matter-of-fact quality in his voice. " What's your name? "

The simple question quieted Janie instantly as no words of mine had been able to. She opened her eyes, looked straight at him, and answered naturally, " Janie."

" Well, Janie," he said, " how old are you? "

" Eighteen," she told him.

" That's just the right age, Janie. You'll have a boy sure," he said, patting her on the shoulder. " Now you just go ahead and have him — you're keeping us all from our beds. Miz Ripley," with a jovial wink at me, " ain't used to it. If that boy's not here in half an hour we'll go home and leave you. Git up and bear down," he ordered her.

A paroxysm of pain went over the girl's pasty face.

(131)

She began to shriek again. Dr. Samson jerked back the bedclothes.

" Wrong presentation," he said rather pompously as though he aired his knowledge of long words.

Rory was bending over to look. I couldn't bear to meet his eyes. I saw his hands. Rimed with dirt they were, and too clumsy to use on anything except the plow.

" Git me some string, quick," Dr. Samson was saying. I ran to look for some. I found a piece on the mantel, the ordinary kind that grocery shops use.

Dr. Samson made a slip noose in it. He bent over the bed.

Janie yelled. . . . " Heaps of calves born this way," said Dr. Samson. " Shut up, Janie. You listen to me, you hear. If this baby ain't here in five minutes it's goin' to be dead. You work now. Push 'em out."

Janie's cries were those of a stuck pig at Christmas time. Dr. Samson worked on. After a time he said, " Bout six minutes, Janie. Probably dead — your own fault."

My ears rung with the noise. I felt half insane. I caught Janie's arm in my two hands. " Think of all you've gone through with, you fool! " I cried. " Use your strength now. Don't you want a live baby? "

It must have been very shortly after that Dr. Sam-

(132)

son straightened up. The terrible screams stopped. Janie had fainted.

Dr. Samson held the baby up by its limp feet. It dangled like a hairless rat. "Dead," he said, "but we'll do all we can. Get something to put on your lap, Miz Ripley, and sit down."

Rory laid an old blue shirt over my knees. Dr. Samson put the tiny creature, blue and limp, on it. He showed me motion by motion what to do with its arms — bring them up over the head, fold them across the breast. It was the same movement as resuscitating a drowning person, I think.

Dr. Samson had gone back to Janie. I hoped I wasn't going to be sick. I couldn't help thinking that the thing on my lap looked grotesquely like something dressed to be roasted on a spit over the fire. I knew I'd be sick presently, I who hated to go into butcher shops, who couldn't bear to see the chickens flopping about after Sarah had wrung their necks. I am not of the stuff nurses are made of.

It was nearly an hour that I held that mite in my hands, working its arms up and down. It occurred to me in my state of overwrought nerves, "Why, I have the power God has. Maybe by doing this I can call this soul to life. If I stop it will just be one of those that never was at all."

I began to play with the idea. I looked at Janie, at

(133)

uncouth Rory. With the life before it wouldn't it be better for it not to come alive? There are so many babies in the world already nobody wants. It's a kind of pity for people to feel so definitely they must have their own. Why not take a poor little kid that's already here and give it a chance? What's the use of cluttering up the world with so many babies anyway? Poor little babies, unwashed, badly fed, their little noses running with colds through the winter, growing up to be field hands in the long, hot days, or maybe going through something like what Janie had just been through.

All the time I kept working its arms up and down. The doctor was through with Janie. He spoke to me from across the room:

" Ain't in your line, eh Miz Ripley? " There was a condescension in the tone that made me feel impotent and humiliated the way being spanked did as a little girl.

I was looking at the doctor and still trying to think of something to say when I felt rather than heard the faintest of noises. It was the most detached, the most eerie of sounds. It was a soul that complained of being born and clung to the outer world. " Dr. Samson," I whispered — I hardly dared move my lips — " I do believe it is alive! "

Dr. Samson turned sharply. He came over to me in three strides. He took it off my lap. He worked its arms, rhythmically, carefully, ruthlessly. I was so excited I could feel my own arms working with his in the empty air. It looked like a baby now. Its cheeks had color in them, its voice was a quite distinct faint wail. Dr. Samson dangled it once again by its feet. The wail became a true cry.

" Oh, Janie," I said, " it's alive. The baby's all right." I was standing by the bed.

Janie raised her head from the pillow. " Is hit a boy? " she said eagerly.

" No," I answered. " A little girl."

" Oh," she said. She shut her eyes.

Dr. Samson wrapped the baby in another old shirt, this time a white one. " Got any cotton? " he said.

Rory said, " I'll go get some." He went out into the field around the house to see if he could find a few bolls that might have been overlooked when the crop was picked. He brought a little in and Dr. Samson turned his head to say " Pick out the seeds first and then git some lard to grease this baby with."

Rory greased. I tried to turn away from his chinless face, with the beads of sweat standing out on the forehead, at such close quarters.

I dressed the baby in clothes I found on the bed. There was no flannel, only a cotton band. I laid her down beside her mother.

All the while I held the baby Rory had been watch-

(135)

ing me. I had supposed he looked so worried and sad because he thought the little thing was dead. I glanced toward him now. His face wore the same expression of dejection but he nodded to his wife — " You can't help hit, Janie, that hit's a girl."

" Well, Pa," said Dr. Samson, " Where's a drink for the old doc? "

Rory jumped like a jack-in-the-box. He fumbled under the bed and brought out a jug and a tumbler. He poured the tumbler half full of white corn and the doctor drank it and handed it back to him. Rory solemnly poured a drink for himself.

I took up my coat. " If there's nothing more for me to do, Doctor, I'll go now," I said.

Dr. Samson turned about sharply as though he suddenly remembered me. " Sure," he said. " Ain't much used to births, eh Miz Ripley? " he chuckled.

I opened the door and the cold dark met me like a long lost friend.

Rory followed me to the door.

" Rory," I said, " you've two fine girls in there now, a big one and a little one. You ought to be proud of them."

" Yes, ma'm," said Rory.

" Rory," I said in a burst of generosity, " tomorrow I'm going to send you down some soft cotton and some baby clothes and Warren's old crib for the baby to

(136)

sleep in." I felt magnanimous for Warren was still using the crib, and Rory knew he was.

Rory's face took on a vacant, rather sullen look. I never knew whether he was overcome with gratitude and embarrassment or whether he was resentful at having to accept charity. "That'll be all right," he said.

I went home and took a bath in the cold dawn. I shook Clem awake. "Get up," I said, "Janie and Rory have a daughter, and the funny part is I borned it just as much as Janie did."

Clem said, "Stop laughing that way — what's the matter?"

"Clem," I said, "I hate these damn people. Oh, Clem, I never want to see any of them again."

14

One spring day Old Man Britt came up with his own scrubby brown mule to break ground for the vegetable garden.

Warren was a friendly little thing. Before I could stop him he toddled over to the mule and clasped his foreleg tight in his two arms and laid his cheek against it; " Mimi," he whispered, an ecstatic expression on his face. Warren called all soft things Mimi after our cat.

I managed to keep presence of mind enough to walk over to him slowly and pull him away gently, so as not to startle either him or the mule.

Old Man Britt was chuckling. " You look pretty white, Miz Ripley," he said. " That mule won't hurt him none, the young 'uns climb all over him."

It was as simple a thing as that but for the first time I really felt the grip of the farm on me. Brought up on a farm my child would have to learn to know the work animals intimately. Almost from now on he'd play with mules and cows and later with trucks and tractors and stationary engines. I couldn't let myself be afraid of the mules kicking him or the cows hooking him or of his catching his hand in the machinery. I picked him up and let him pat the mule's soft nose. I wished I had learned to know mules when I was Warren's age as Old Man Britt had.

Old Man Britt broke the ground for the garden. I chose a new place as we hadn't had luck with our garden last year. We laid out between an eighth and a quarter of an acre. I noticed brown and lifeless Bermuda grass growing on the place I chose but I had no conception of its potentialities.

I planned for Lacy and me to take care of the garden. Clem had the dewberry crop to attend to, and he was taking a course in short story writing besides, his second and third stories having been returned to him with rejection slips.

We didn't have to wait long for the garden to sprout. The whole place, vegetables and weeds began to sprout at once. Lacy couldn't, or wouldn't, tell the difference between them and pulled them up indiscriminately until I reluctantly admitted to myself he did more harm than good and I'd better take care of it alone.

(139)

The rabbits were a nuisance. One early morning Warren and I were hoeing as usual — in the carrots, I think — when I caught sight of one nibbling at the end of the third row of green peas. I frightened him away with the hoe. "That makes me tired," I said in a tone of thorough irritation. I wouldn't have said it if I'd thought because I knew Warren liked the rabbit. Most of his books had pictures of rabbits and they were generally the heroes of the stories.

Warren looked thoughtful but he didn't say a word. A day or two later Mimi, the cat, dragged up to the house a little rabbit she'd killed. He and I saw her from the window. I was afraid his feelings would be terribly hurt. "Bad Mimi," I said, "to kill the poor little bunny."

Warren's mouth turned down but he said sturdily, "No, Katti, it's a good Mimi. Bunnies are what makes people tired."

It was funny and a little pathetic. Close to nature you learn early to dispense with sentiment. Warren and I used to watch the rabbits sometimes dancing and playing about sunset between the rows of the orchard but after that day in the garden when the rabbit ate the peas and he thought that was what made me get tired he always looked at them most reproachfully and dis-approvingly, especially if we'd just been struggling with the weeds.

(140)

We got a lot of peas after all. Lacy and I would pick in the hot sun until my head was swimming. The Bermuda grass was bad. No matter how carefully we pulled it, the fragile roots broke and from each break a new blade sprouted. The spring plowing had just given it a good cultivation.

The string beans were a moderate success and we had good luck with carrots. I hoed in the early mornings and I hoed in the late evenings and I picked at midday when the sun glare on the sand made the line of the horizon turn cartwheels in my brain.

It was such dull work. It brought no money in. It saved us some intangible amount; I never could figure just how much but I know it was very little. But Warren needed plenty of fresh vegetables and I consoled myself with the thought that he was getting much better and fresher ones than we could buy. We saved too on the gasoline for a few trips to Pinehurst. I stuck to it because I had started but I knew I was silly. . . . As nearly as I could figure I was putting in my time at the rate of about five cents an hour.

" All this work," I said, " and I've saved about ten dollars in all, a man's time for five days in the orchard."

" That's what I've been telling you," Clem said. " But you would butt your head against a stone wall. Your time is worth more than five cents an hour to

(141)

you if you don't do anything more with it than powder your nose before the mirror."

But this seemed such a pleasant way to reason. I was sure it must be wrong. I am not so sure now — although at that time we were hard up and ten dollars looked big to me. Nevertheless, ten dollars could not make any real difference in our year's living and I was earning it in a way that was most difficult and unpleasant to me. It was teaching me nothing that would be of service on the farm in a commercial way, either.

I didn't spend much time powdering my nose in front of the mirror but I spent lots, especially at night after I was in bed, trying to think things out. Here I am, a girl who's had first and last a good deal spent on my bringing up and education. If I'm going to work this hard, surely I ought to be worth more than five cents an hour, I reasoned. I tried to tell myself I liked it — to watch things sprout — to watch them grow a little bigger each day. And I was interested in them. But then I'd remember that we just picked them and ate them up and they were gone, but my nails were still split from grubbing up Bermuda grass and my face still ached from the fine particles of sand ground into it when I hoed. I still had a cramp in my back and a headache from bending over in the heat.

Lots of roses grew about and over our house. All

(142)

I ever did to the vines was prune them. I'd choose a pleasant day and I liked doing it. That hot summer I'd stare at the rose vines, which were covered with flowers and never seemed to be troubled by pests. " All I'd ever like to have to do with gardening," I thought, " is to pick roses."

But there was a domestic high spot in that summer: our twenty-seven baby ducks. Warren and I had always taken care of the poultry. Warren collected the eggs in a little basket. We were fond of the hens and chicks but we fell absolutely in love with the ducks.

We used to sit together on the sand in front of the house and feed them. The mothers stood at a respectful distance but the babies would run up my arms and jump into the bowl in my lap. This impertinence used to outrage Warren and he'd discipline them with the spoon.

We filled a big washtub full of water and we'd put them in to swim. They looked perfectly mechanical.

Warren and I loved them, and we played with them, and did everything for them all wrong. In spite of it, all but three of the twenty-seven lived, a far better record than we ever had from ducks afterwards when we had learned how to handle them scientifically. When I think it was I who was so ignorant in those days I can scarcely believe it.

Again the dewberries didn't really pay. We had

(143)

a good crop but the express rates were high and the price was low.

Our gang of children solemnly struck for a cent and a half a till and won the strike. Warren and I picked some and when we counted the red-bug bites on us at night I sympathized with the strikers.

Oh, well, year after next when peaches are ripe — I'd watch for shooting stars at night when we sat on the terrace wall to cool off after the long hot day. When I saw one I'd try to say " money, money, money " before it died. I could never say it all before the star went out, but I wasn't superstitious. Peaches were still money to me and our orchard was in splendid condition.

15

It was lonely when we came back from the North in the fall to do without the Birds, but we consoled ourselves with the thought that they would live at Pinehurst and not move entirely away from the Sandhills. Their orchard had been bought by a group of men in Candor solely for the peaches. They had put in a foreman to run the place but no one lived in the dwelling house. We found we drove over more and more to Pinehurst for recreation.

The winter orchard work had become a routine that Clem knew thoroughly and that even Rory was beginning to understand. Clem struggled all winter with his writing and sold several stories to thriller magazines.

The few hundred dollars helped eke out the living expenses. When the spring of '24 came we had still between four and five thousand left and only a year to go before next summer and our first peach crop.

" I'm going to plant cotton in the old melon field this year," Clem decided. " Probably I won't make more than a couple of hundred dollars but it's the safe, sure crop."

And I said, " All right. Everybody has to try cotton once. Better get it over with now."

Clem asked me what I meant.

" Only," I told him, " that nobody in the South has much respect for sand land cotton and that the melon field is a pitiably small acreage. . . . But I want a crop of my own," I said. " Give me two acres of land and the labor and seed, and I'm going to try Baby Delight watermelons."

I had had a few Baby Delights from a friend's garden last year and it struck me they ought to be a knockout commercially. Baby Delights are an almost perfectly round, dark green watermelon about the size of a man's head. Inside they are a brilliant red and deliciously sweet. If you happen to be Southern there's enough watermelon for two or if you're Northern they'll serve four portions, or even six maybe.

Oftentimes in the market I've seen housewives hesitate over the size of a melon. " It's so big," they'd say. " My family can never eat a whole one up." But when the greengrocer showed them a smaller melon, they'd say, "It looks immature. The last small one I got wasn't ripe."

(146)

It seemed to me that the Baby Delights filled a long-felt want. A perfectly mature Lilliputian watermelon.

I engaged old Amos Britt by the day. Watermelons are an easy and cheap crop to grow. They take very little fertilizer and cultivation. Few pests attack them. If you hit a good year when the market's right you may make a lot of money on them and if you hit a poor year you can just leave them to rot in the field and you lose comparatively little.

From the very start my melons grew beautifully. They were small enough to pack in honeydew crates and we had plenty of those left over. I wrote to the various commission men I intended to deal with, in Washington, Richmond, Norfolk and even New York, explaining what the melons were. When they began to ripen we packed the first few and sent them off. They were the darlingest looking, little dark green watermelons in miniature — it seemed to me I was bound to make something out of those melons.

I still don't see how the public resisted them. But the commission men wrote back there was just no sale for them — the jobbers didn't want to take a chance on a new thing. They were hardly bringing express.

I felt very badly over those melons. Clem, to comfort me, offered to take a few truck loads up to Greensboro or Raleigh and hawk them through the streets.

(147)

I was sure if people would just get over their prejudice against them and try one they'd like them.

Clem and Rory and a full load left early Saturday morning for Greensboro. I would have gone along for my heart was in my crop if some people with a letter to us from Clem's father hadn't been planning to drive over for tea that afternoon.

All day long I thought about Clem and Rory and the melons. I hoped they might go like hot cakes and Clem get home to meet his father's friends at tea time.

But the guests arrived and still no Clem. They were rather formal people, two men and a woman, old enough to be my parents. They drove up in a big car with a white chauffeur.

I was glad I had changed my dress and that I'd conquered in the battle of the shoes with Warren. He was clean and shod even if he did cordially invite the chauffeur to come in and join us, much to the latter's embarrassment. " Katti," he said, " always likes gentlemen."

The house was cool and dark after the glare of the sand country. Lacy brought in a silver pitcher of dewberry cup, which is not unlike claret cup and really is very good. Lacy didn't own any shoes but he had on a white coat, a heritage from Leo, which, though it swallowed him, was spotlessly clean. The pitcher

(148)

was almost as tall as Lacy but he took himself very seriously as a butler and carried it with as much dignity as possible under the circumstances. If you can't have your servants well trained and efficient you may as well have them amusing. Old Sarah, a huge symphony of black flesh, blue linen and white cambric, hovered solicitously in the background.

One of the men, the one who I knew had been in the diplomatic service, commented on Lacy when he had gone and everyone had smiled behind his solemn little back.

" There is something almost oriental in your little black boy with his big pitcher," he said. " But he's not the proper atmosphere for you. You'd be right strolling in a picture hat between the trim box hedges of a formal garden. You are very Southern, aren't you? "

I thought of me a few hours before toting Baby Delights through the melon hills but I smiled like a lady.

" I'm sorry," I told them, " that Clem had to go to Greensboro today."

They said that they were sorry, too. And the lady asked agreeably, " Did he motor up? "

I nodded — why explain?

"A lovely day for motoring," she said.

" Yes," I answered, " Clem enjoys it very much."

(149)

" Does he drive an open car? " asked the diplomat.

I thought of the truck with no top or windshield. " Yes, indeed," I answered brightly and a little nervously — they were very fancy people. I thought, well I'm in for it now. I may as well be hung for a sheep as a lamb. I waved my hand toward the orchard and farm. " This," I said, " is his avocation. My husband is an author, you know."

They were obviously interested so I began to elaborate. It had been a dull day. These people are rich, I thought. Everyone I know, nearly, is rich. I'll never see these people again. For the afternoon I'll be rich, too. I had a lovely time. I was just explaining that the farm was a sort of Petit Trianon, and wondering if that wasn't spreading it a little too thick, when my ears, trained to the quiet of the country, caught a sinister sound.

It was unmistakably the rumble of the truck down the road and I knew Nemesis was upon me.

There was no use trying to head Clem off. Warren had heard the truck too and dashed out calling, " Clemmy, Clemmy!" Clem came through the door with Warren on his shoulder.

He wore overalls, of course. That would have been enough, but it was far from all. He was dust and grease from head to foot.

" Those damn melons of yours," he was saying,

(150)

" the load was too heavy for the truck and on the way home we had two blow-outs."

I forgot all about the guests.

" On the way *home?* " I gasped. " Didn't you sell *any* of them? "

" Sell them? " said Clem. " You couldn't give them away."

Simultaneously we remembered the guests. All three of them were convulsed with laughter. Even the chauffeur, who could see and hear us through the open door and windows, wore a broad grin.

The ice was well broken. Clem washed his hands and had some dewberry cup, and the guests seemed our age, and we had a jolly afternoon.

When they left we loaded the car full of Baby Delights. I heard from them afterwards and they said they were the best melons they ever ate. Of course, the gentleman had been a diplomat.

Clem's cotton came on later. Cotton is generally planted in our section on the share-crop system but Clem decided to pay his labor outright and take the entire crop. He was to discover it was much the most expensive way.

Cotton is essentially a darky crop and the cotton farmer who makes a profit out of it is the landlord who grows it on shares. The chief item in growing a cotton crop is the labor. The cotton must be planted, cultivated, hoed or " chopped," interminably. Then it must be picked. All these are simple but endlessly tedious operations.

The darky tenant works in the crop with his wife and all his family from children eight years old up. In the fall when the cotton is ginned and sold he gets a third for his labor. The landlord who had supplied the land, the fertilizer, and the " furnish," which is a small credit for groceries at the country store, and which he, of course, deducts from the tenant's share, gets two thirds.

Comparatively few darkies are capable of figuring the value of their own time and that of their families. If they were, they would probably discover they were getting far below the current wages for day labor. But the darky doesn't know. At the end of the crop he gets his money all in a lump in his two hands where he can count it. He likes, too, being his own boss and having his little farm to himself.

In the mind of the tenant farmer there is the vivid memory of the year cotton went to forty cents. That was during the war. It will probably take another war to ever get it there again, but the darky is a gambler and a confirmed optimist. Cotton has gone to forty cents once, he argues. This is the year when it will go there again.

The darky (and poor white tenant, too) is usually

(152)

so ignorant and hide-bound by superstition and suspicion that the old reliable cotton crop, which he understands how to plant and cultivate, is the only safe crop to trust him with. We've hired many men, white and black, who believed implicitly in the influence on crops of the phases of the moon and the signs of the zodiac. Cotton should be planted on a waxing moon, melons and fruit in twins (Gemini). Corn planted before the moon is full will run entirely to stalk and make practically no ears. Government bulletins may argue in vain. The poor whites and the blacks in our section know how the old folks did it.

In dealing with labor of this class it is better to give them some crop simple to handle and something that they and their fathers before them have grown. That is one of the chief reasons that the South clings to cotton, in spite of the boll weevil, poor prices, and the pitfalls of the one crop system.

From the small landlord's point of view the share-crop is the only system for cotton planting. Except for a very occasional outstanding year it simply does not pay to hire labor to plant cotton. This is certainly true of North and South Carolina and Clem only learned for himself what more experienced growers had told him.

We didn't make much cotton. It cost us fifteen cents a pound. The quality was not first rate either.

(153)

Sand land cotton seldom is. We netted less than a hundred dollars on almost ten acres.

"Is there nothing," we wondered, "this country will grow but peaches?"

We decided this must be so. Certainly there were no rich general farmers about us.

16

Clem worked that peach season for Mr. Maurice. He handled the loading of the cars. He checked the truck loads as they came to the siding from the pack-house. He attended to the re-icing of the bunkers. He wrangled with government inspectors on the quality of the fruit and the rating it should have.

"There are going to be no slip-ups when my crop comes in," he told me. "I'm going to learn this peach business from every angle."

'24 was a queer season but then every peach season is different. No grower can ever look ahead or count his profits before they are actually deposited in the bank. Sometimes it isn't safe then if they are in a Southern bank.

'24 was an unusually late season. South Georgia was shipping Elbertas heavily when the Sandhills' Hiley Belles and Belles of Georgia began to come in.

Sandhill growers got very much less than they had counted on for their Belles this year, but they consoled themselves by thinking that the Georgia crop must be nearly through and we'd have the market to ourselves for our Elbertas and the price would shoot up. But the days slipped by and the cars continued to roll from Georgia and the price instead of going up dropped.

Most of the growers were startled. Georgia was so much farther south than we, how could their trees bear so late? It had never happened before. But it was happening now and there was a perfectly reasonable explanation. In previous years Georgia's crop had come from south Georgia but this year the late fruit was coming from the high lands of north Georgia where the season is just about as late as the Sandhills' season. It was from new orchards just beginning to bear. South Georgia had finished shipping but north Georgia was our direct competitor.

Roger Derby's prophecy was beginning to come true.

A few growers like Roger philosophically looked ahead to the lean years and talked and wrote in a vain endeavor to discourage the planting of new orchards but the main bulk of the growers persuaded themselves, I think, that '24 was a fluke.

It was the lateness of the season, they said, that threw Georgia and us together. It had never happened before — it probably wouldn't happen again. Those orchards

(156)

in north Georgia were planted too high. Their fruit would be killed in the winter.

In the Sandhills we kept on planting orchards. Even Roger put in a new block. But if one is a peach man one must. A commercial orchard only lasts about fourteen years. You must have new trees coming along to take the place of the old ones. You cannot replant each individual tree as it dies because little new trees will not grow where an old tree has stood and between other mature trees. You must plant a fresh block, timed to come in about when your old orchard goes out, if you are to continue in the peach business. This was not expansion but replacement.

But the speculators in real estate who had bought sites for orchards still tried to prop up the boom. They and the local newspapers felt, " Let's get the people here, tell 'em about money in peaches and thus we'll build up the section." There were heaps of bona fide Q. W. Ertys still.

The situation troubled Clem and me. All we had was sunk in our peaches, and after the season of '24 we could not expect to sell our place for anything like what it had cost us. There was the same trapped feeling as I had had the night Warren was sick and we drove down what we hoped was the Perseval Road. Once started the road was too narrow to turn back. We could only creep ahead and hope it would turn out all right.

" I doubt," Clem said one day in the fall, " if we'd better count on our first crop too much. Next season may not be any better than this. Suppose we just figure on the crop paying the farm expenses for '24 and '25, how much will that leave us to live on? "

We figured that at two hundred dollars a month we had barely enough to last us through the winter.

" H'm," Clem said, frowning. " Well, of course, I can borrow to run the orchard next winter, and for picking and packing '26's crop. I hate to borrow for living expenses, though. I'll just have to write better paying stuff, that's all — try for the high-brow magazines."

" You made about six hundred dollars last winter out of your stories," I reminded him, though heaven knows we both knew the figures down to the last nickel. " You're bound to have learned something about writing. You ought to make at least twelve hundred this winter, don't you think? "

" Yes, I do," Clem said. " I'm going to write a different type of story from what I've been doing, too. Write about things I know, Pinehurst, resort people in contrast to the country people out here — real life."

Clem, that winter, in his grandfather's chair, hunched before the fire with his typewriter on his knees. A cold north wind that moaned down the chimney and sneaked in under the French doors. And me darning

(158)

the holes in socks and stockings and wondering what I could do to make some money. I'd been asking myself that question a year now.

Many of the socks and stockings had holes in them, past darning. I used to put the mended socks and stockings in one pile and those that were too far gone to be mended and that Warren had outgrown in another. Above the fireplace, where I couldn't help but see it every time I happened to look up, hung a soft colored, old hooked rug. I don't know how long it took two and two to make four in my mind.

Hooked rugs were made by women like me with plenty of time on their hands through long winter days and evenings. They made them on burlap and undoubtedly out of old clothes too worn to be mended. I got some empty fertilizer sacks from the barn. Sarah washed them and I began, with a crochet needle and the old socks and stockings, to hook rugs.

The first rug I made had a ship on it sailing on a stormy sea. I had lots of black stockings so I made a school of dolphins follow the ship. There was a bright orange sock of Warren's and I made a running light on the ship and a moon to shine above it. I worked on it through long, quiet evenings while Clem read aloud to me what he had written through the day. I enjoyed improvising the pattern and seeing the rug grow under my hands. It cost me nothing to make and when it

(159)

was finished I sold it through an antique shop for eighteen dollars.

I found I could sell all I could make and I liked to make them. All my friends saved their old clothes and stockings for me. Every bureau drawer and closet bulged with rags. It is slow work though, making rugs. I spent several weeks on each one. Taking my time, for the number of hours I spent, I was getting about ten cents an hour. Less than unskilled field work. In all I made only about a hundred dollars out of hooked rugs, through a year or so.

Unlike gardening, hooking rag pictures on burlap was fun. But it did not solve my problem. Even eighteen miles out in the country there must be something I could do that would pay.

In casting about for something I could do I naturally thought of driving about the country and picking up antiques and bits of Americana that I could resell at the same shop that sold my rugs.

The first bit of Americana that it occurred to me I might buy and resell was native pottery. This was an entirely unoriginal idea as lots of people had done or were doing it. But most of the people I met seemed to be interested in native arts and crafts and waxed enthusiastic over Moore county pottery. There was a shop full of it in Greenwich Village. There had been a recent article about it in *Country Life*.

Until a few years ago most of the dishes and churns and like articles the sand and clay people used were made on a kick-wheel by one or another of the local potters. They say the first potters came from Staffordshire and the trade was handed down from father to son. Even now much the same kind of pottery is being made by their descendants, although tourists have suggested many innovations which the potters call "toy ware," but which they make to sell at filling stations and shops.

One day I drove the twenty-five miles to the best and cheapest potter I knew. I bought ten dollars' worth. The car was full to the top with jugs and bowls and toy ware.

I priced it triple what I had paid for it, packed it in barrels of pine straw, and consigned it to various gift shops. Most of it sold but I made very little out of it after I deducted my gasoline and wear and tear on the car for the trip, the man and truck's time to haul the barrels to the station, and the express (the stuff's heavy). After that I bought pottery every time I had occasion to go by one of the potters but it brought only pin money and did not pay to make special trips to get it.

Even more dear to the hearts of our friends than native arts and crafts were antiques. Surely, I thought, through the country I can find lovely old pine and

(161)

walnut pieces in an old section like ours. I knew through labor we had hired from time to time, many of the country people. Janie had a cousin who had an old corner cupboard. Amos knew an old lady back in the clay who had a clock with wooden works. Lacy's contribution was a friend who had a real old-time sewing machine.

The corner cupboard proved to be twenty-seven miles away. Fourteen of those miles were back country clay roads. The Chevrolet stuck hub deep in the mud. Ellen Maurice was with me. Fortunately, we had two jacks and we burrowed down in the mud and jacked up the two rear wheels. With the help of a clay-dweller with a team of mules who happened by, we got it out. But a few miles farther on we stuck again and this time it seemed to be for good and all.

Fortunately, we were just opposite the cousin's house. We left the car and went in to ask to see the cupboard. The cousin was alone on the farm. She proved to be a sour, deaf old woman, with a snuff-stick hanging out of the corner of her mouth. The cupboard was back in the shed, she said, and she took us out to see it. It stood there, big and clumsy. It was nothing but rough pine planks nailed together, possibly twenty-five years old.

We all went toward the house together. Ellen and I were hungry. It was long past luncheon time and our car seemed to be stuck until the boys, as the old woman called her sons, came back from the sawmill where they worked. That would be probably about sundown. The old lady went on " God's time " and the mill, she said, ran on " sawmill time." It seemed to be a great grievance to her that they couldn't agree on what time the sun set. She wouldn't give us a bite to eat. She said she had barely enough for herself and the boys. She said we might come in and set though if we had a mind to.

We followed her inside and there in the front room I spied the chest. I squeezed Ellen's arm. It was a homemade walnut chest with the ends dovetailed together, well proportioned and not too big. I nudged Ellen. She whispered, " Worth thirty dollars in any shop."

" How about selling me that chest? " I asked.

" Well, now I don't rightly know ma'm. I ain't ever figured 'bout it. Hit's a useful chest. Hit's just right fer my quilts."

" Yes," I said. " That's so. But look how old it is. I'll give you five dollars for it and you can get yourself a nice new trunk from Ward's instead. You'd like it much better."

The old woman hesitated. " I reckon you're right ma'm. I know hit's old and kinder no-count," she said a little bit crestfallen. " But I'm used to that old chest."

(163)

Her eyes narrowed as she looked at me. " Hit was my grandma's," she ended with pride.

" Then it's time you got a new one, isn't it? " I said, with a smile.

" What you want hit fur? " she asked. A little pig was nozzling in at the door. He grunted at her inquiringly. " Shut up, you! " she screamed. She shook her fist.

She turned back to me. A suspiciously wheedling tone crept into her voice, " What you want with hit? "

" Why, I don't know. I happen to like old-fashioned things," I answered. " I'm just foolish that way, I guess." I laughed a little to show how foolish I was.

" Well, ma'm," she drew herself up. She said positively, " If you want hit I want hit." And that ended it.

I was rather relieved. I'd done my best to get it and I'd failed.

Just then we saw a group of boys and girls coming down the road on their way home from school.

" Come on, Katti," Ellen said, " They'll help us push the car out."

On the way home I said to Ellen, " I'm kind of glad she didn't sell me that chest. Why should I make six hundred percent on a chest that old lady really likes because it was her grandmother's? I'm darn sorry I ran it down, too."

(164)

All the same I might have gone more intensively into antiquing if there had been more good pieces in the section. But the hardy Scotchmen, who followed Flora McDonald to the Sandhills, couldn't have had much with them but the shirts on their backs. The older houses I went into were generally furnished with beds laced with rope, some of them old but rough and homemade, a shelf or so for pots and china, a deal table and a few split-bottom chairs.

Generally the people were most hospitable and glad to see me. Lots of them had heard of me. I remember an old lady in a frilled white cap, who told me she was over a hundred years old. She spoke with a strong Scotch accent and we were friends from the first minute when she opened the door, asked who I was and exclaimed: " Mistress Ripley! Why did ye no bring your baby? I like babies."

She gave me a cutting from a lavender bush that came originally from the Highlands, she said. The cutting lived and is a big bush today.

It was she who told me of an old prayer book, either she or one of her friends had. I couldn't make out which.

" It says different from some prayer books now. It says ' frae ghostes and ghoules and lang-legged beastes and things that go boomp in the dark good Lord deliver us.' "

(165)

I'd love to have seen it but how could I have offered her money for her prayer book even if she had shown it to me?

I found instead of buying antiques I was making friends with the people and telling them about the Exchange at Pinehurst where they could sell their home-made brooms and patchwork quilts and crocheted bedspreads and make a little something for themselves.

My reason tells me it isn't so — that it is just a coincidence — but bread cast upon the water often does come floating back in totally unexpected ways. When I acted as packhouse foreman in our peach crops I could always get labor. Girls and women came to work for me who wouldn't be bossed by a professional packhouse boss and they were generally a higher type than the average and more dependable.

"You know that day you come to see us at our home, Mrs. Ripley? Pa says we couldn't work for no Georgia cracker but we could come to you."

Perhaps as much as my own distaste for antiquing, an episode that occurred with a pair of beds that I bought in the country discouraged me.

I found them about twelve miles from home. They were too big to go in the car. I persuaded Clem to drive over in the truck the next afternoon to get them. We filled the tank up to the top with gasoline. We thought we had allowed plenty of time for the trip but it took a

(166)

long time finding the woman and a long time to dust off and load the beds.

We hadn't gone more than a mile or so on the way home before it began to get dark. The truck was old and it had no lights. Clem drove as fast as it would go to try to reach the highway before it got too dark to see the road. We were on a fairly good country road, about three miles from the Maurices' place.

Warren was sitting between us. He had on a warm coat but he was wearing socks and his knees were bare.

" I'm getting awful hot," he complained.

" Hot? " I laughed. " You mean cold, boy. Even in woolly gloves my hands are cold."

" I sure am so, hot," Warren said doggedly. " My legs are hot and my eyes hurt."

I bent over to see about him and at once my eyes were stung, too. I smelt a queer burning smell.

The truck was making a lot of noise. I nudged Clem. " Better slow down, Clem, the engine's pretty warm," I said in his ear above the wind.

Clem jammed on the brakes and stopped short. All about our feet little flames shot up.

Clem grabbed up Warren and caught my arm. " Jump! "

The next instant we were out in the cotton field. The little flames were licking about the floorboard of the truck. We didn't know how long it had been burn-

(167)

ing. As long as we were going the wind had blown the flames and the smell back. I remembered the full gasoline tank under the seat.

I dragged at Clem's sleeve, " Come on," I shouted, "before it explodes."

Clem was staring at the truck. He put Warren on the ground. " The insurance has run out," he said. " I haven't got a thousand dollars for a new truck." He snatched up a handful of sand and ran toward it. As he jerked away the seat the flames shot up six feet in the air.

" Run, Warren! " I said. " Quick! "

" Katti," he screamed in terror and clung to my skirt.

I shook him. " You run! " I said. " You want to get burned up? " I gave him a push to get him started.

Clem was scooping handfuls of sand and throwing them on the blaze. It was absurd when I knew we might be blown to atoms any second, but I was glad I was wearing heavy gloves if I had to handle wet sand.

" What if it blows up, Clem? " I panted.

Clem denies it now, but what he said, between handfuls of sand, was, " That would be very disagreeable."

It couldn't have lasted thirty seconds. A lucky

throw of sand caught the big blaze and put it out. The little ones were easy after that.

We were standing by the still smoking truck and Warren was clinging to Clem's trouser leg when a car drove up and stopped.

"Whee! Smell the smoke!" said the nice boy who got out. "Need any help, Mister? There's three of us here."

"No thanks," Clem told him. "We've had a little fire but it's out. I wish you'd drop my wife and baby by the Maurices', though."

"Sure, brother. Hop in, lady."

I couldn't speak my heart was beating so fast.

I was still out of breath when we got to the Maurices' place. I told Mr. Maurice about the fire. He left in his car with a fire-extinguisher to go pick up Clem and put out any smoldering embers.

Warren hadn't cried or said a word since that terrified "Katti." We had been half an hour sitting in the drawing room with Mrs. Maurice and the girls when I said, "Are we keeping you from your dinner? They ought to be back by now."

Warren looked at me with big eyes. "Katti," he said in the tone of a grown-up explaining to a child, "Clem is burned up by now." And he couldn't be persuaded otherwise.

I've never seen anything like the joy, surprise and

(169)

relief, that were that poor baby's when Clem came in at last.

After all there was not much damage done. There was so much gasoline in the tank it hadn't had time to get very hot. We bought a new seat and did a little patching and the old truck was not much the worse for the accident.

But my antiquing ended literally in a burst of flame. For months afterward Warren would sniff suspiciously whenever we were out in a car.

17

The winter months slipped by. Rory and Clem got the pruning and spraying done, and Clem polished his stories. They weren't bad stories, I thought, but they all came home over and over again with rejection slips. They were about our neighbors in the country and in Pinehurst, but the editors thought they didn't ring true. Clem was discouraged. In the spring he told me, " I'm through writing. I'm just a plain farmer, I guess. I'll stick with the peaches."

Half a dozen times a day I would walk through a few rows of orchard and stand rapt in admiration before the little swelling green peaches. Our first crop!

Mr. and Mrs. Butler had gone abroad to live after last year's disastrous prices. Young Benny, the old gentleman's son, who was about Clem's age, was running the orchard. Since the war he had been working down in the West Indies. He was bronzed like a Richard Harding Davis hero and he had the kind of sense of humor seldom found outside of Wonderland. Benny hadn't a penny except an interest in his father's crop. For him peaches had to pay in '25, too.

And '25 was a hot summer. All day long the sun rode, a red hot disk, across the sky. The tortured trees drooped in the heat. Rory with the two-horse plow cultivated back and forth across the orchard in an effort to force a little moisture to them from the parched soil. The little peaches hung small and lifeless on the branches.

Benny had a way of showing up at our house just before noon with a flask of corn in his pocket. "Let the sun cross the yardarm, damn him, and we'll have a little drink to rainy day."

It made us nervous and fidgety to wait day after day for the rain. In the older orchards the peaches were beginning to shrivel. Our fruit on the sturdy young trees stood the drought better. "We'd be all right," Clem kept saying, "if only it would rain."

Benny had worked hard all winter. He had given up all the parties at Pinehurst and been out at daylight every morning with his darkies. He drove the tractor himself and saved a man's time. It had been a startling change from the Benny of a year before who used to get home in evening clothes of a morning in time to wave his hand to his father's foreman starting pruning, as he drove

(172)

past on his way to the house. Benny's orchard was three times as big as ours. His old trees were not standing up well in the heat but he had a large block of young ones in their second bearing year, which were in fine condition.

"I know each peach personally," Benny said. "If we can only get a rain they'll be as pretty as any fruit that ever went out of the Sandhills."

Georgia packers coming up early to pack the Mayflowers and Carmens used to sing,

> "Rain makes the corn to grow,
> Corn makes the liquor flow,
> Lord, let it rain."

There was a humming from white and black everywhere — at the store when we drove over for the mail — a snatch of song from the fields as we passed by — from an open cabin door —

> "Tain't gon rain no more, no more,
> Tain't gon rain no more."

May and June went by, half of July, and still the pitiless sun shone down, burning up the crop.

Benny came over to our house on one of the hottest afternoons I ever felt.

(173)

"Let's drive over to Jackson's Springs and go in swimming," he said, "I can't stand looking out at the orchard and seeing what this is doing to the fruit."

Jackson's Springs was one of those black, still-water ponds, dammed up long ago to turn a mill wheel. We had it to ourselves this afternoon. Warren paddled along the bank while Clem and Benny and I swam lazily in the milk-warm water. We could see heat lightning playing over the distant horizon as we pushed our way through the coiling waterlily stems.

It was practically without warning except for the dimming of the sun by a huge smoky yellow cloud across the western sky that the first real lightning came. It was a wide jagged streak of fire that seemed to hit the far end of the pond. At the same instant there was a deafening crash of thunder. Tiny ripples broke across the glassy surface of the water.

We turned and swam for the shore. Another flash of lightning and roar of sound as the heavens cracked a little and big drops of rain dotted the pond.

I was where I could stand by now. I grabbed Warren up and ran into the tumbled-down mill.

The lightning struck the pond. A tree near us was hit. The lightning played on the dynamo of the mill. The rain was a blinding sheet of water between us and the pond.

(174)

I hadn't realized I was cold until I looked at Benny. He was blue and shaking with a chill. I said, " Let's get out of here."

We ducked our heads and stepped out on the narrow dam. The wet clay made us slip and slide as we tried to run toward the road and the car. The distance was hardly a quarter of a mile but lightning struck the dam behind us twice before we reached it.

Benny's chill was the result of malaria contracted in the tropics but we were all chilled and blue, still in our wet bathing suits, for it was a cold rain. Shivering and with chattering teeth we sat close together.

The road was a red river of mud.

" God," Benny said, " if my teeth'll just keep quiet long enough I'll sing You a song of thanksgiving. When You send rain, what I mean is You send rain."

It was twelve miles to Benny's house which was six miles closer than ours. The blessed rain had stopped as we drove over but it seemed to get colder and colder as we got nearer his place. Benny's orchard was beyond the house but we stopped the car in the scuppernong vineyard. We all four of us were chilled to the bone, but, half frozen as we were, nobody protested as he knelt down in the sand and began to dig.

" It's gone fairly deep," he called to us. " It surely will sink to the roots of the trees."

We laughed and grabbed each other's wet hands. We all talked at once through chattering teeth. Benny's peaches were saved.

He found some clothes for us and we had a drink. I couldn't wait any longer. I was sitting on the edge of my chair with impatience.

"Let's go see if our orchard got the rain too," I said.

Everybody was on the highway or in the village as we drove through. Several men called to us but we didn't slow down. It was only because we needed gas that we stopped at a garage.

A lean countryman slouched up to the car. "I'm mighty sorry about your orchard, Mist' Butler," he said, "the hail hit you mighty bad, didn't it?"

Hail! I kept my eyes on the radiator cap. Hail! A colder breath than the chill air seemed to creep toward my heart.

"I — I haven't seen my trees really," Benny was saying slowly. "Has it been hailing here?"

A group gathered. "Sure has," somebody said. "I reckon your young trees is pretty near all pecked up. Harrison was hit hard right acrost from you. Mister Jesse Page ain't hardly got a sound peach. The Maurice orchard wasn't hardly touched, though. Seems like it just skipped him."

I tried to shut out the buzz of voices. I tried not to listen. But I heard them say at last what I dreaded.

(176)

" Seen your orchard, Mist' Ripley? The hail come from over that-a-away. Samarcand's hit bad."

They poured in the gasoline. We drove on in stony silence. No wonder people were driving the road. We saw now what in our joy and excitement we hadn't noticed before. The orchards that lined it were wrecks of leaves, broken branches, and fallen peaches.

Everywhere men were wandering through them, estimating the damage, shaking their heads, kicking aside broken limbs.

Samarcand was hard hit. The wet sand under the young Elbertas was littered with little marble-like green peaches. I turned my eyes away.

We turned into the woods road toward home. Something seemed queer. I missed the new washed smell of trees. I looked well at the road. It was hardly wet at all. I looked at the blackjack and pines. No water dripped from their branches.

We came out into the orchard. Clem was out of the car before it stopped. Rory was wandering about looking at the ground under the trees.

" Hail hit us, Rory? " Clem called.

" Hail? No sir," said Rory. " Nor yet rain neither. Just a few big drops or so to pepper up the sand, and the storm went t'other way."

The cold wind lifted a cloud of dry dust in our orchard. Clem and Benny and I looked at last at each

(177)

other. We began to shake with a kind of hysterical laughter.

When I could catch my breath, I said, " God don't hardly ever aim to hit a man."

Benny said, " Hasn't He a remarkable sense of humor, though? You can't beat God."

Clem said, " Yes, but it's the last time I'll ever go into a business where I've got Him for a partner."

Only Warren whimpered, " I'm still cold, and I can't find my hands in Uncle Ben's coat."

18

The Sandhills growers had had a coöperative association for marketing their fruit. It had not been a success, due, it was generally conceded, to the fact that no single association can keep tab on all the markets. It requires a large organization to keep in touch with the prices paid and the number of cars received in all the cities. Our association functioned in this way only through the peach season.

The obvious plan then was to employ an agency which had a large enough capital and organization behind it, and which functioned for a variety of crops throughout the year. The American Growers, whose trademark is the Blue Goose, came in and took over the business of the section. Here and there an individual shipped independently, but the American Growers handled by far the bulk of the crop.

The grower consigned his car to the American

Growers, Potomac Yards. They marketed it for him, taking eight percent gross on all f.o.b. sales and ten percent on all other sales.

In theory, if New York had more cars than it could handle and Hartford less, the American Growers were aware of this and your car went to Hartford. Since obviously you cannot go with each car to its destination and sell it yourself, it seems reasonable that a central organization can handle the marketing better than if you consign the cars to individual commission men at random, as we had the express shipments of dewberries. It is a far from perfect system but so far it has been the best offered to the growers.

The American Growers lent us the money to buy crates and pick and pack our crop.

The rain we prayed for never came. Once or twice a " drizzle, drozzle " for a few minutes, or a pitter-pattery rain that sprinkled the sand with big round drops. Slow, tired rain that seemed to stop from sheer inertia in the heat. The cultivation kept the trees going. The fruit was much smaller than it should have been but it was reasonably good. When it began to color up and show signs of ripening, Clem wired the Georgia packers he had engaged to come up. This being our first crop we wired them in plenty of time to have them on hand when we needed them.

The man, Brown, had been a foreman packer and

(180)

was a good judge of the quality and condition of fruit. We paid him six dollars a day, his wife, also an expert packer, four dollars, and twenty-five dollars each for transportation in addition to their food and lodging.

Their first day we only had twenty-five crates ripe for them to pack. Brown and Mrs. Brown with evenly sized, carefully graded peaches should have been able to put up close to a hundred crates a day apiece.

Brown was an experienced crate maker and we set him to work making crates. The crates come knocked down. We had bought enough material for fifteen hundred in case we should have a larger crop than we expected.

There was nothing for Mrs. Brown to do. If she had been a native girl we could have sent her into the orchard to pick and saved a man's time, or she could have worked as long as there was work to do, then gone home, and been paid only for the number of hours she put in. But she was a professional packer. She had been hired to pack. If there were no peaches ripe enough to pack that was our lookout, not hers. She sat idle and her pay went on just the same.

Next day we had only fifty crates. Clem suggested Brown go on making crates while Mrs. Brown packed, but they didn't see it that way. Brown said he had plenty of crates ahead and he'd been hired to pack. The

(181)

two packed the fruit in the morning and through the long afternoon while Brown went back to crate making Mrs. Brown crocheted.

By the end of the week we had only got about three hundred crates in all, and the Browns' wages and transportation amounted to a hundred and ten dollars.

Janie had said she had so much to do, what with the baby and all, that she couldn't board the Browns, so I had to feed them at the house. They slept at Janie's, but three meals a day for a whole week I had watched Brown's fat hairy hands shovel food to his loose-lipped mouth and had listened to Mrs. Brown's nasal Florida twang as she recounted her triumphs with the boys — before, " Mr. Brown jest took me offen my little tootsies and married me whether I wanted to or not. I never did say ' yes,' did I, hon? "

Brown would respond to a sally like this with a "Now, hon! " then turn to me, his face beaming with pride despite a mouthful of potatoes. " She's jest like a baby girl, ain't she? " She was easily thirty, and had two gold front teeth.

They were very nice about it when they were fired Saturday, the end of their week. Brown agreed there was really not enough work to keep them occupied. I had the promise of a job for them in a neighboring orchard. Mrs. Brown simpered and said with an arch glance at Brown: " Better watch wifey, hon. There'll be

(182)

plenty of good looking fellers packing there, I'll bet you."

I told Clem when he came in what I'd done.

" Do you think you can handle the rest of the crop, Katti? " he said. " You know, I'll have to be with the pickers and running up and down the road trying to arrange for somebody to ship with."

I said, with girls to help, I was sure I could. I had been watching the Browns and learning from them and I had no doubt of my ability to pack at least fifty crates of fruit a day myself. With two girls to grade and help pack we could certainly easily handle seventy-five. Seventy-five was the most we had got in a day so far.

I was up at the packhouse at six Monday morning. Brown had made up over a thousand crates so I didn't have to worry about that.

Three red-cheeked girls were there waiting for me. Minnie had packed last season at Samarcand. She said Mr. Ripley had promised her two dollars and a half a day, wages. Cherry had only graded and she was to have two dollars. They had brought with them Annie, a little ten-year-old cousin, in case I could use her. I promised Annie a dollar a day if she would paste the labels on the crates and run errands and fetch and carry.

Clem had promised that later on one of the pickers could come up to nail on the crate tops.

It was eight o'clock before the wagon creaked up with

(183)

the first load. Old Amos Britt was driving. A darky boy named Sam was with him. The two unloaded the oblong picking boxes on to the platform. They had twenty of them.

" This and one more good load'll wind up the Belles," Amos said.

The boxes were piled almost level with fruit, delicate green and shell-pink Belles of Georgia, with the dew just drying on them. They shone and glistened with a kind of virginal radiance. Not ripe enough to eat, not green enough to hang another day on the limb without softening. Belles picked to ship always make me think of —

> " Johnny Jones and his sister, Sue,
>   Ate a peach of emerald hue."

I'm sure it was a green Belle they ate and I can readily understand the temptation.

" Ain't they pretty, Mrs. Ripley? " Minnie and Cherry exclaimed in chorus.

Sam lifted the boxes to the grading shelf. We graded them by hand. Annie helped and we four went through the load. The fruit was evenly sized. The drought had kept it all small, a two-two pack, despite the tendency of young trees to grow large fruit.

I was the slowest grader. Even little Annie finished

her boxes before I did mine. But I couldn't resist letting each peach linger in my hand. I'd rub off the fuzz that dimmed the color side. I admired each perfect curve from the crease where the stem broke to the delicate pointed, yet rounded, tip. Each peach with a soft spot or a blemish gave me a conscience-stricken pang. Could it have been avoided? Had we left something undone? I found one worm-hole and it was such a calamity and somehow disgrace that I saved it for Clem to see.

Sam nailed on the crate tops and we were all through and passing the hot forenoon eating soft peaches when the wagon came up with the second load.

Amos had thirty boxes for us this time. " And there's more full boxes in the field ready to come," he said. " We're getting more peaches than we figured, stripping these Belles."

Stripping means pulling off all the fruit that's left on the tree. A little may be too green but this is sacrificed as there is usually not enough to make it worth while to pick over the tree again. Some of the fruit is always soft when the tree is stripped as once a tree begins to ripen up it comes very fast. There are always, too, undeveloped peaches and oddities that have been overlooked in previous pickings.

The grading was harder now. It was a hot day. The sweat trickled down our faces, flushed from bending over the grading tables. When the girls put up their

(185)

hands to brush their hair back from their foreheads a faint red rash showed where the fuzz stuck and prickled. The smell of ripe peaches hung in the packhouse.

We managed to finish up the Belles by noon. We got forty crates in all.

A load of Elbertas was in the packhouse waiting, ready for us to begin on, when the lunch hour was over at one. If the Belles had had a pale loveliness the Elbertas were flaming beauties. Looking at them I felt refreshed. Warm, rich, rounded, yellow and dark glistening red. I forgot how hot I was and that my clothes stuck to me. There is an elusive fragrance and gloss to newly picked fruit which wears off in a few hours. It wears away so gradually that you hardly know it is gone until suddenly the fruit looks dull, the shine is not there any more. It's the same subtle difference between newly cut flowers and those that have stood in a vase overnight. It isn't so noticeable in a small quantity of fruit, but a whole packhouse full has, when the fruit is fresh from the orchard, a sort of indescribable glow.

" It's a strange thing, Mrs. Ripley," Cherry said. " They don't look as though they'd be fuzzy neither."

Since the trees had stood over since Saturday we knew there'd be plenty of fruit to come today, but I wasn't prepared for more than half of the whole Elberta crop at once.

Clem, who had been with Rory and the pickers all

morning, came up to the packhouse to tell me about it early in the afternoon.

"Katti, I'm going over to Samarcand to see if I can borrow some packers. We'll get two hundred crates today."

We were swamped with fruit. Annie helped grade and Sam nailed and pasted labels, too, but we couldn't empty the boxes fast enough for Amos, who kept bringing in full ones from the field. Clem picked up a couple of packers from somewhere and stood by to lift picking boxes and cull baskets and to trade with cull buyers who happened by. The pickers finished in the orchard and when they came up to the packhouse to drop their baskets we put them to work grading.

Fortunately we found a place for the fruit in a Samarcand car which was to be held over until the midnight train. We packed until dark and finished just as the light failed so entirely we couldn't tell which side was color side.

My eyes burned. Peaches swam before them — endless rows of peaches — beautiful with a malignant, fascinating beauty. My back and shoulders ached. My hands were sore. But it was nothing to the pain in my feet. I doubt if I'd ever stood all day long on them before. Even in bed that night the soles still ached.

I went to bed as soon as I got home and had had a bath. Sarah brought me my supper. She had the grace

(187)

to apologize for the sliced peaches and cream for dessert.
" It do seem too bad not to use 'em though."

I thought of the bushels of culls still unsold in the
packhouse and I thought of the bushels of peaches still
hanging on the trees. I thought of tomorrow — and
tomorrow —.

But that was the worst day. There were not many
ripe next day and the extra girls we hired stood about
practically idle until noon. Three more pickings and
we were through. Seven hundred and forty-two crates in
all. A very short crop.

We wondered if our expenses had been higher than
they should have been. We had had more pickers than
absolutely necessary except on our one big day, Monday.
And the short, slow ripening crop had not warranted
the Browns as packers. Another year we were sure we
could gauge better. But when Clem talked the matter
over with other growers and heard what they considered
necessary we felt our cost had not been excessive.

With a perishable crop like peaches it is very difficult to estimate from day to day how many to expect.
If you do not have enough labor the day your fruit is
ready to come you may lose quantities of it. When it
begins to ripen, it comes on fast, but a cool day may
delay it twenty-four or even forty-eight hours. Warm
rain on the other hand sometimes brings the whole crop
on overnight. Once your gang is there, you must pay

(188)

them half a day's time whether they work or not. It just takes lots of experience in handling a crop to know ahead of time how many hands to engage each day.

From the day I let the Browns go I packed peaches, I think, as cheaply as anyone in the Sandhills. But I never had enough people and we were almost always in a push, always just getting the last load to the car as the engine was about to pick it up, and having to beg the engineer to wait a few minutes longer while we locked the doors. Yet we did get the crops off and a penny saved is a penny earned.

I found last year when we had a professional foreman handle our packing, a good man too, that he demanded more girls and men in the packhouse than I would have dreamt of having for myself. But I doubt if in any business you can hire a man to put up with the inconveniences the owner will. There's a reason for this, at least it was so in my experience. Every two dollars a day, graders' wages, I saved and every two and a half, packers', I could translate into clothes and trips and amusements. Or put it another way. Every extra dollar I spent might mean doing without some luxury we had grown accustomed to; enough might mean doing without the necessities.

As far as money went we never had much leeway. There was a sort of pride, too, in doing the job cheaply,

(189)

in putting out a good pack for less than you were told it cost other people. I hated the actual work of the pack-house, but there was a kind of thrill to it that dragged me back to it each year. A fool idea that other people would make mistakes, that no one else could pack our crop as well as I could. Certainly no one else could have been as interested in it as I was.

When the returns came in we found we had averaged net only about a dollar and a quarter a crate, making a total, including the small amounts we had taken for culls, of about eleven hundred dollars.

Our crate material came to three hundred and thirty dollars. We had only used half of it of course and the rest would keep until next year. Our packing, picking, and hauling (we had traded in our old Ford truck for an almost new Chevrolet truck) came to about four hundred dollars. We had had borrowed money to run the farm during the winter. After we took our crop expenses out we had about three hundred and seventy dollars to meet a thousand dollar note.

We had to live. We put the three hundred and seventy dollars in the bank and renewed the note.

Other years the failure of melons or cotton or dew-berries had been annoying. But we had always felt that these crops had just been a gamble and we had lost. Peaches were our real business. When our orchard came in the lean years would be over and we could have the

(190)

things we had waited for and done without. And now our first peach crop was a failure too. Far from helping toward our living expenses it hadn't paid for the labor and fertilizer to produce it.

The drought had made our fruit small and so it had taken more peaches to fill the crates, but that was not the main trouble. With a normal crop (a crate to the tree) it is generally admitted you can break even on a year's crop expenses with a dollar and a quarter fruit, but this leaves you nothing for interest on your investment or to tide you over a bad year. In all our figuring on our orchard we had counted on an average of two dollar fruit year in and year out as a minimum for a reasonably paying proposition. That is, three dollar fruit some years possibly, and a dollar and fifty cents fruit other years, but the general average not to drop lower than two dollars. The year we bought our land several growers told us that they averaged four dollars.

The glaring fact staring at us was that we had received only a dollar and twenty-five cents for our fruit. There had been too many peaches in '25. The market had broken again.

The explanation was that more north Georgia orchards were coming into bearing. We had no reason to expect anything but worse prices in '26 than we had had this year.

(191)

We could offer our orchard for sale, but everybody's orchard was for sale and no buyers. I doubt if we realized how poor we were. In debt and going further in to produce a crop a year away that we were pretty sure would result in a deficit.

19

And yet when I look back I don't think I ever enjoyed any summer of my life as much as I did that summer after our first crop failed. Ned and Willie Beall were living then at Samarcand. Ned had been in the Foreign Legion and with a romantic war record and a good game of golf and bridge he had been always in demand at Pinehurst. Now he was tiding himself over to some vague future as Raphael's bookkeeper. Willie was the sort of girl you like on sight. If you'd committed a murder you'd naturally choose Willie Beall to confide in. They were both tolerant and amusing and very much alive. They had with them a young Italian, Paul Franco, who had finished three years at Oxford a year or so ago and who was most delightfully British. There were others who came over occasionally from Pinehurst and the other orchards, but these and Benny were the people we saw most of.

We used to play poker through the long hot August nights with a ten-cent limit. For us to lose ten dollars was cataclysmic. We were all broke together. I doubt if millionaires get as big a kick when their stakes are hundreds of thousands. After all if they lose they won't have to save it by a week's economy on food.

The dewberries might not be a commercial success but prohibition never troubled us. " Everybody," Warren said once, when he was philosophizing on country people not having running water, " has wine and corn liquor and milk."

It was a summer when all of us lived entirely in the present, for none of us knew we'd do in the future. As Benny remarked, apropos of Ralph Page's county families, " We're the discounty families now — all people of note."

A summer when there's no use worrying because there is nothing you can do about it — a summer picked up with pincers from the rest of your life, when everybody talks and laughs and wise-cracks and does crazy things, because they don't like to look back at the immediate past and they're afraid to look forward.

Cool swims in the millpond and picnic suppers afterwards and long drives in the car. Ten-year-old motion pictures in a sort of tent at one of the villages. Benny and Clem urging me to go without stockings and

(194)

smoke as I went in so they could watch the outraged expressions on the people's faces from back over in the clay.

> " I've got sand in my shoes,
>   I've got sand in my hair,
>   I couldn't get a price for peaches anywhere.
>   It's a funny monkey business,
>   Living on a farm,
>   Another little drink wouldn't do us any harm."

One moonlight night, and Paul diving in and out over the little hedges in front of our house shouting, " It's the Grand National, boys, it's the Grand National."

" Do it again, Paul! "

This time he landed flat on his face on the brick walk. He picked himself up with a reproachful look and explained with dignity, " In England they don't run it on bricks."

I remember the evening my serving canned peaches for dessert started an all-night argument as to what we'd each order for dinner if we could have anything we wanted. Most of our food that summer was canned. The gardens lay parched and withered in the drought. Benny and Ned pounding the table over the relative merits of a filet mignon and a horse bucket of steamed clams.

(195)

Paul's elaborate wine list. Clem's ultimatum — " I'll stick to corn."

Atta boy, Mr. Q. W. Erty! Boost home industry!

" I've got sand in my shoes,
   I've got sand in my hair,
   Going to a party and got nothing to wear.
   We can't sell the peaches,
   That we grow on our farm —
   And another little drink wouldn't do us any harm."

Here we go on the red dog's back! Two bits on a black card.

Hot days and warm still waters to swim in. Cool nights and white moonlight on the sand outside almost as bright as the lamplight indoors. Careless laughter and long arguments over world questions that never got anywhere and crackled and sputtered in the fireworks of wise-cracks. And all that we saw about us was ours. Nobody's radio next door annoyed us. We did as we chose and there was no one in the apartment above to ask us please to make less noise. Who wouldn't sell a seat on the stock exchange and buy a farm?

Well, it had to end, of course. The Bealls moved away and Ned went into business. Paul went out to the oil fields to make his fortune. Benny went to California. Clem and I stayed on the farm.

(196)

One day in October Clem said, "A classical education must be good for something, and, you know, I think I know what it's good for. It's bunk to pass along. I'm going to see if I can get some tutoring to do in Pinehurst this winter."

I said, "If you must enter a life of shame, go to it."

Milton Bird had always been interested in child psychology and in how children's minds work. He was a great help. He had done some tutoring himself and he recommended Clem. Clem brushed up his Caesar and geometry. Through the winter he got several pupils.

We were honest to goodness poor now. Clem's old overcoat was so shabby he used to take it off and leave it in the car before he went into somebody's house. And yet poverty is relative. We gave that same overcoat eventually to an old colored man to wear to his son's funeral, and he felt he was magnificently dressed and it was a great consolation to him.

But poor or not we had a lot of fun. That was the Christmas Eve that eight of us were together at a dance at the Carolina Hotel. Nearly everyone was in fancy costume but us. We took turns in impersonating bears in the five fur coats we had between us. We thought we were very funny. There was a party in a room upstairs. Somebody insisted on having a Frigidaire installed then and there to keep the drinks cold. I remember the bland resignation on the face of the mechanic as he fitted it up.

A lot of people drove out to our place to spend the rest of the night. All of us in evening clothes shooting Roman candles over the orchard to welcome the dawn. A true daughter of the South I had fireworks on hand. I'd had them for Warren but he was spending Christmas with my family.

When I was a child in Charleston we always had fireworks at Christmas. Christmas Eve the grown people set them off to amuse us. Flowerpots and skyrockets. Huge Chinese fish with flaming tails floating over the housetops. And last of all the steady burning Star of Bethlehem, brilliant, serene, warm and friendly, floating away in the dark sky.

The warm covers pulled close about my chin. Stay awake and catch Santa Claus creeping down the chimney. The bicycle I wanted — the doll — the mint candy walking stick that would hang on the tree. But always just before sleep caught me the big glowing Star of Bethlehem floating away in the cold blue night.

The clear, sane instant when you stand aside and see yourself and the people about you in a stark white light. When the years behind you have faded and the years ahead are dark.

Snap out of it! This is a party. Oh, Baby, are you cold? Grown people trying to be children again. Escapers from life. Somebody sing. Somebody build up the fire. Everybody have another drink!

In January Gloria Swanson and her company came to Pinehurst to shoot some scenes. Somebody gave a party for them at the Country Club and the younger married crowd went. There were only twenty or thirty couples but we had the whole Club to ourselves. It was all hung with velvet curtains. There were two orchestras. One of the girls who belonged to the troupe had a thing she called " patine " plastered thick over her face and arms and legs until she looked like a mulatto. When she got up to go in to dinner there were fourteen empty cocktail glasses standing in neat rows under her chair. It was that kind of a party.

Gloria's director had been at college with Clem. His wife and I clicked at once. She was going up to New York next day and had engaged a stateroom for the trip. This, she explained, necessitated buying two tickets. She invited me to come along and go up with her.

It had been a long time since I was in New York. It was a chance to see the plays and the shops. I wanted to feel the pavement under my feet, even to smell the smoke and gasoline fumes, to be in a crowd of people. I had a good many friends in New York and several of them had asked me to stop with them any time I went up. . . . " Or," the girl with the patine suggested in

(199)

a burst of enthusiasm, " you can live in my place in the Village — I've lent it to a couple of Russian princes but they'd love having you."

There was a thrill in looking through my things to find what would do for city clothes, in looking back and seeing the farm disappear in the turn in the road. There was mixed with it a vague apprehension, a lack of self-confidence. For besides the anticipation of the holiday I had a more serious reason for going.

New York is the big market. New York sets the prices for produce. I had a list of commission men in my bag. I made up my mind I was going to see them and talk to them — try to find out what it was all about if I could.

I felt almost as though I had landed on Mars when Fredericka left me at the Pennsylvania Station. She was going on to Greenwich. I had my return ticket and about thirty dollars in cash.

I knew the trip was an extravagance if it was just for fun and a rank gamble if it was for gaining market-ing information. I'd made up my mind that thirty dollars had to do me. Frankly I hoped the people who had invited me to stay with them would take me to theaters and things. At any rate I could call on my com-mission men, and do some window shopping before I had to go back home.

I went into a telephone booth and began to call up

my friends. The first girl I telephoned to was out of town. The second had moved.

The rush of people back and forth and the crash and bang and shuffle, of the station, made me feel as though someone had taken me by the shoulders and whirled me round screaming, " Hurry, hurry! "

After the leisurely flow of time at Samarcand, where every question inevitably brought forth the deliberate, " Well, I dunno as I could rightly tell — " which gives you a chance to think before the answer comes, the quick jerky answers these people here shot back at me confused me. My ears attuned to slow Southern dialect didn't catch half of what they did say.

New York wasn't the way I remembered it. I wanted to run — to find someone I knew — to leave this bustle and space for the four walls of a room that would shut out the noise.

The only other person I could think if I could ask to put me up was Philippa Richardson. Her number was not in the 'phone book. I asked Central.

" We are not allowed to give Mrs. Richardson's number," she said, clipping off the words primly.

I remembered that pernicious habit of New Yorkers of having their numbers only in the Social Register. I rang Central again. I tried to explain. But there's nobody so rigidly impersonal as a New York telephone operator.

It all seemed so silly. Here I was in New York after

(201)

all this time, and because a telephone girl was a little unimaginative automaton, I'd have to go home again tomorrow. I had no illusions about how long thirty dollars would last me at an hotel.

It was already late afternoon. I could see one or two commission men in the morning and take the three-thirty train south.

On an off chance I asked at the information desk if they had a Social Register. They hadn't. I looked about the station. Even if no one actually touched me, I felt jostled in this clattering, banging place. I was used to being treated with a certain deference in the country. I was somebody there and I liked it. I found myself pulling my coat tighter about me and standing as straight and tall as I could.

There was a boy lounging in front of one of the tele-phone booths. He was about seventeen years old, with a pimply face and a green suit of clothes. He reminded me of a Georgia peach packer dressed up for Sunday. I had been aware of him for some time in the same ab-sent-minded way one is aware of a table or a chair. I almost jumped when he deliberately winked at me and took a step forward.

Suddenly I wanted to laugh. Here was this funny child actually trying to pick me up. It was the same scene I had watched so often between Georgia packers and country flappers.

I walked quickly into the station. I began to feel impersonal again, to look at the place *en masse*. . . . " Even though you're such a noisy place," I thought, " you really haven't been in this world as long as I have." . . . The people scurrying about and running up and down steps reminded me of ants running in and out of holes in the ground. They had the same look of feeling important and harrassed. I regained a sort of detached viewpoint. I remembered Philippa had a husband. His name was Charlie. . . . It takes Charlie such a long time to get to his office in the mornings. . . . Charlie has to go — has to go way down to — to — Charlie has to go way down to WALL STREET! That was it.

I went back to the telephone booth. The boy in the green suit had gone. I began to look up Richardsons on Wall Street. I couldn't believe my luck. There was a C. E. Richardson and Somebody listed.

I called them and a pleasant voiced girl said, " Mr. Richardson is busy. This is his secretary. . . . Yes — Yes —" surprised, " Mrs. Richardson's name is Philippa. . . . You're her cousin? . . . Or, your child and her children are cousins! Oh! "

My words tumbled over one another in incoherent explanation. I was afraid she'd hang up. And all the time a perfectly sane portion of me was standing aloof, a little ashamed.

(203)

Was this me, frightened and ill at ease as a child? I jotted down the number and called.

A half hour later, over tea and toasted anchovy sandwiches, I asked Philippa, " Have you ever heard anyone else say this town made them feel as though they were on a ship? I mean the height and the noise and the rush and all makes me feel stumbly, the way the deck of a ship does. Do you suppose I'll get my sea-legs? "

Philippa laughed. " Let me give you some tea," she said, " and we'll talk about what you'd like to do and see while you're here."

She laughed again when I told her I had come on business — that I had to plan first of all to see the commission men. I was telling the honest to God truth, but I knew it would affect other people just as it did her. And, come to find out, I was right.

I spent a week in New York and I went down to the wholesale district and talked, or tried to talk, to various jobbers and commission men. Whether another woman, one who looked older and knew how to go about it better, would have had more luck, I don't know. Undoubtedly a man would have commanded more attention. But nobody took me seriously. And nobody seemed to give a sweet damn about my peaches.

The feeling of being whirled about and having people shout, " Hurry — hurry! " in my ears grew stronger as I trudged from office to office. I was just

(204)

nothing. I knew I seemed futile. The men I talked to were mostly minor clerks. I suspected that some of them thought me a little demented — that I really didn't have an orchard at all. They were polite, mildly puzzled, and obviously uninterested. As a matter of fact I don't think they really knew what I was trying to get at. I was anxious to find out what the jobbers wanted. If for instance they thought it would be worth while to spend the extra money to grow a superlatively good peach, one to sell only to exclusive shops and hotels, and if our orchard was big enough to satisfy a demand for this class of fruit. Or if a special kind of fancy package would help. Or if they had calls for any certain number of peaches packed separately.

But if they ever had demands for anything out of the ordinary in peaches the men I talked to didn't seem to know about it.

I knew I was pretty ignorant but if this was the center of our distribution, the headquarters of market information, I had got to, then heaven help the peach industry.

In spite of plays and shops and people and parties I was bitterly disappointed. I had counted more than I had admitted on what I could learn in New York, on some particular hint on how to market that would enable us to sell our peaches, if we could grow just what the trade wanted, even in a year of overproduction.

Clem met me at Southern Pines. On the farm there was plenty of trouble. Laddie, the little water spaniel, the Bealls had asked us to keep for them, had got his foot caught in a fox trap and had lain there four days. The poor little fellow was too weak to walk when a farmer a mile away found him. Clem had taken him to the veterinarian and he had cut off two toes.

Some pipes had frozen and we had no running water.

Clem was bothered over the damage the sleet had done to his winter oats.

Old Sarah had a misery in her back and a bad cold.

And halfway from the Southern Pines station to the farm we remembered we'd forgotten to get the meat and the canned goods on the grocery list.

Very much more than six hundred miles of track separated me from New York.

20

As usual Clem and I were avoiding the subject of money.

Old Sarah was working for five dollars a week, and Lacy for his board and clothes — real peonage. The roof leaked and we patched it with tar. A chair broke and we put it away. Through all the years I can't remember replacing anything but bare necessities like brooms and soap. When a sheet tore I mended it, and when it tore too badly to be mended again, we had one less sheet and Sarah used it on the ironing board or to help out the flour sacks as dishrags.

I had quantities of linen and silver to begin with, and what I had I used. We had tall silver goblets. We used them for water. We used them for milk. We used them for everything. They tumbled off the table or sideboard and were battered and bent but they did not break.

We used silver for everything we could and saved the china and glass.

Old Sarah loved the silver. Sarah had won a prize when she was young, for the best polished silver at the fair. That was when she was working, for Mrs. Judge Tyler, " 'way up in Virginia, where I was born ma'm. . . . One time Miz Tyler put her finger in the sausage grinder. We was grindin' sausage. It done took a finger off. She never blamed me, ma'm, but she looked at me so queer sometimes, I was glad to go."

Sarah polishing the pitchers with a chamois rag, flip-flip, not very fast, and telling Warren, now he was old enough to like stories, all about the Tyler children back in Virginia, and about 'possums and 'simmon trees, and the burying society she belonged to, and about her own daughter. Long pointless tales that made Warren's eyes grow round as saucers while the silver reflected him and Sarah, and the pots and pans on the kitchen wall in its shining depths.

One of the pleasant things about farm life had been the rich milk and cream and the home-made butter. For a long time I suspected we paid city prices for our thick cream and milk. There is comparatively no pasturage in the Sandhills and our cows had always been practically entirely stall fed. This winter we decided the cow was a luxury we couldn't afford.

The Samarcand Dairy had failed, but we found we

could get milk from the former dairyman who still kept a cow for his own use. We began buying butter in Pinehurst. We ruefully admitted when we compared the figures that it was a substantial saving.

Leaving out the original cost of the cow and Rory's time in caring for her, the cost of feeding her had averaged about fifteen dollars a month. Buying milk and butter cost us about that, but when the cow had gone dry or calved she ate just the same, and we had to buy milk and butter. Also when we were away the cow still ate, and we had no market for the milk we could not use.

We had to admit that, although our milk and butter were better and we had the luxury of cream, we had paid maximum prices for them. We decided that home-produced milk and butter were luxuries we could do without. For us to keep a cow was to be out of tune with the times.

It had been a game as well as a necessity to beat standardization and do things cheaper and as well on our own. Using kerosene lamps instead of a farm electric plant is a real saving, we found. Periodically the agents for farm electric plants used to come to see us. They could show us that you can run the plants for even less than you can buy kerosene, but they were stumped when it came to writing off the original cost. They always ended weakly with, "Think of the time you'd save, not having to fiddle with them lamps." But after

(209)

all, it was Sarah's time that would have been saved, and she had plenty of time. They tactfully avoided the subject of repairs to the plant when I pointed out that a brand new lamp only cost a dollar and fifty cents. But here's something to think about. Our kerosene bill was more for lighting our house on the farm than the electric light bill for the same sized city house would have been using city electricity. Our water pumped with a gasoline engine and an auxiliary windmill, of course, cost ten times as much as city water.

There are advantages to standardization.

When I think of the farm I always find myself thinking in terms of money. The farmer takes each year such a gamble as few operators on Wall Street would dare. He stakes his year's time, his money, often borrowed money, and bets he can beat weather and pests and market fluctuations. The odds are generally against him, but the stakes are large and he may win enormously if everything breaks in his favor. I never happened to know a farmer in real life who genuinely loved the soil as they are supposed to do in fiction, but I knew plenty who loved the gamble of planting crops. Even the small tenant farmer feels this way. He can get a safe job in the cotton mill with a good house, amusements and medical attention, but it is a humdrum job. There is no chance of a lucky break and his wages shooting up sky-high. On the farm this may be the year cotton will go to forty cents and his share-crop make him, according to his standards, a fortune. It's the most fascinating game in the world once you've tried it.

We had borrowed from the bank to finance next season's crop. We thought we were pretty certain to have a big crop our second bearing year and excellent fruit on such healthy trees. Surely, in spite of the quantities of fruit that would be dumped on the market, we'd get a good price for ours. We'd be able to get out of debt and start afresh. There is a curious confidence which buoys up a forlorn hope. It's hard to believe you are going to fail when you need to win so desperately.

The government sent us discouraging bulletins about peaches. They advised growers (three years late) not to expand. They estimated the size of '26's crop and prophesied low prices. The reports from Georgia were that the trees there were heavily set with fruit. Nevertheless there is an excitement that comes every spring with the buds bursting into bloom, and that spring was no exception.

One morning when the orchard was a big pink bouquet, with the vivid green of rye grass between the rows, I nudged Clem, as we drove through on our way to Pinehurst.

" Just look! " I half whispered. " Isn't it simply lovely? "

" The view's probably costing you about a thousand

dollars this season," Clem said. " Take a good look and enjoy it while you can."

Clem believed the government bulletins literally, but I was slow to learn. I couldn't admit to myself that our second crop could be as flat a disappointment as the first had been. I kept telling myself, " Probably they're just a bit pessimistic." I didn't know as definitely then as I do now that the government always polishes and shines up the bright side to show to a farmer. If the government — state or federal — even suggests prices may not be good, then let the farmer prepare for the deluge.

As it turned out, that eye-full of pink and green spring freshness (and nobody who hasn't seen a Sandhills orchard in full bloom knows what the phrase means) cost us nearer two thousand dollars.

The blooms faded and the little long thin peaches formed. Three weeks later they were as big as the end of my little finger. And then toward daylight of the nineteenth of April we had, not a frost, but a hard freeze.

It was a freak season. Not even old Amos could remember a freeze so late in the year. But it killed practically every peach in our orchard. There was nothing we could have done. It was too cold for smudges to help even if we'd had them.

The freeze cut a jagged streak through the Sandhills orchards. Our fruit and that of many of the growers was wiped out.

"If it had come earlier," Clem said, "we might have saved the fertilizer. I'd looked for poor prices, and I knew I might drop even as much as a thousand dollars, but this is our whole year's operation cost — better than two thousand."

"What about the bank?" I asked.

"Oh, they'll carry us on," Clem said. "They've got to. It's their only chance of getting their money out."

There was nothing more to say about it.

The little peaches dropped off the trees. We hired children to pick them up, and had them burned to avoid disease to '27's crop.

Look out of any window of our house and you saw the orchard rows, the trees that had to be kept up whether they bore or not. We knew if we stopped caring for the trees, let them go even for one season, we stood an excellent chance of losing our whole investment. The orchard was a hungry arrogant animal that demanded food — food — food.

Clem had got out his typewriter again, now the Pinehurst season was over and the boys he had tutored gone. He used to sit with it on his knees staring into the empty fireplace — at the rug — at the wall — anywhere but out of the windows.

I still had a pride in the strong trees. They were well

(213)

pruned, round and shapely in full leaf, but for this year I knew they were drones. I made excuses to myself. I loved the farm.

" Well, never mind," I said to Clem —

> " Safe upon the solid rock the ugly houses
> stand:
> Come and see my shining palace built upon the
> sand! "

Clem said, " Take a look at your palace's foundations some day. They're rotting away."

And Clem meant it literally. Sure enough, the floor joists were rotting and we had no money to have them replaced.

I knew he was really depressed. It wasn't like Clem, who is always more optimistic than I, to remind me, when I was trying to be funny about the situation, of some petty trouble.

There was no chance of any real money coming from the farm for more than a year. Meanwhile it had to be taken care of and the orchard was much more expensive to run now it was in bearing. We had to live until then, too. Nothing we had tried to do as a side line in the way of farming had paid. Without simply kissing nearly thirty thousand dollars good-bye, we couldn't just leave and Clem try for a job somewhere. We had the bull by

(214)

the tail, and we couldn't let go. I could tell by the hunch of his shoulders and the weary look on his face when we turned into our road driving home from somewhere that Clem was beginning actively to dislike the farm.

One day Warren said, " I think it's funny 'bout the Walrus and the Carpenter —

> " ' They wept like anything to see
> Such quantities of sand.
> " If this were only cleared away,"
> They said, " it *would* be grand! " '

Why, Katti? "

I said, "Don't you like the farm, Sonny? "

" Yes," he said. " But when I'm big I'm going to get an airplane and fly away."

I had a kind of maternal feeling toward it. I think I felt something like this: if you had a baby, and while it was little you planned out a wonderful future for it and dreamed long daydreams about its growing up, you'd feel terribly to find when it grew bigger that it wasn't just right — deformed or something. You might realize that it would never do you credit but you wouldn't blame it and you'd still like it. I was beginning to suspect the peach orchard was my half-witted child.

(215)

21

" Banker ridin' in the pullman cyar,
 Merchant ridin' in the same,
 Farmer ridin' on the couplin' tongue,
 But it's ridin' just the same."

For a long time we had spent practically no time
away from Samarcand except for sickness or other necessary reasons. If we were going to have a vacation this
was the year to take it.

We got a darky to share-crop the few acres of clay
land we didn't need to make feed, in cotton. Rory could
handle the orchard cultivation alone.

It was almost four years since Clem and Warren and
I had driven across North Carolina to the coast, only to
find that we had to turn around and come home next
day. There is something about the waste of sand in
Moore county that keeps you constantly reminded of

the sea. One June day we packed up our clothes and the typewriter, and drove south to a little island off the South Carolina coast.

It was like coming to the end of the world. First the clay road gave way to black dirt and then the dirt to oyster shells. The air smelt brackish. There was a taste of salt on my lips again. Cabins that we passed were no longer weather-beaten, unpainted shacks but were white-washed, with delft blue doors and shutters. I remembered suddenly why.

When I was a child, my colored nurse used to tell me, " Ha'nts and boogermans can't cross blue."

Edging the fields stood great, graciously branched live oaks with hanging grey moss. A still, windless country. To Clem and Warren it was eerie and sad, but to me it was home.

The road narrowed down to a scant twenty-five feet with a white-washed fence on either side. We turned sharply to the right. Straight beyond lay the smooth salt creek. Warren hadn't seen or even smelled tide water since he was a baby. The road ended so abruptly and the country was so flat and evenly laid out in fence and road and live oaks, it didn't seem very illogical when he grabbed my arm and asked in breathless excitement, " Is this where the world stops? "

The Chevrolet rounded the bend. We saw the causeway across the creek and the sand dunes and white-washed island houses beyond. An old darky woman was fishing in the sunny water.

She bobbed us a skimpy little curtsey. " How you, my missus? "

It was the soft, cooing drawl of the tide-water, unbelievably gentle and mellow — utterly different from the up-country darky speech.

We had a one-room cottage, all put together with wooden pegs, on the salt-creek side of the island. There was no glass in the windows, but we tacked mosquito bars across them and pulled the heavy shutters to when it rained. The high tides crept up under it, and tiny fiddler crabs crawled through the cracks and scuttled back and forth across the floor. Once or twice a big wharf rat peeped at us from a corner with bright, beady eyes. We could hear the boom of the surf across the dunes, not a hundred yards away.

On still nights we'd walk or lie on the beach and count shooting stars. I have never seen so many. Or we swam in the surf and the phosphorous outlined our bodies in pale fire.

There was a boarding house where we had meals — almost all sea food — served on a long, spotlessly clean, pine table without a cloth. There were other little boys for Warren to play with. They had fiddler races and sailed boats on the salt creek, or picked up shells and

(218)

built castles on the beach. . . . Only Warren built barns and chicken houses, and stuck bits of seaweed, spaced evenly, for peach trees.

Except when we went bathing or to meals, Clem pounded all day long on the typewriter. There was a story he began for Warren one hot night. It was about a desperate gang of men, modern pirates, catching seals up in the cold waters of the Behring Sea. Warren liked it so well that the next night Clem continued it. Night after night it went on and on. It even got a name — Smoky Seas — from the deep fog that shut in over the little sealing schooners and tricked friend and foe alike in the fierce battles over the stolen fur.

" You know, it has quite a plot now," Clem said one day. " I knocked out a sort of an outline of it on the typewriter — a fight to every thousand words. My realism hasn't gone, and I think I'm going to try thrillers again."

We had been away from the farm over a month, when a letter came from Roger Derby. He was in the midst of his crop, he wrote. Nemesis had come to the Sandhills. Growers were getting returns of seventy-five cents or a dollar a crate, and the price was still dropping. It looked as if it would hardly be worth while to pick and pack the crop.

Roger had a plan for Clem to go North at once and

(219)

try to sell his peaches direct to resort hotels. He offered him a hundred dollars and expenses.

We talked it over.

Clem said, " I don't believe it would work. The trouble is the season's so short. Suppose an hotel takes a crate or two as an experiment, to try. Maybe they like them fine but by the time they have finished those few crates enough time has been lost so that it's too late for them to order many more. The season's just too short for that sort of thing."

" Yes," I said. " But it wouldn't take you but a couple of weeks and a hundred dollars is a hundred dollars."

" That's just how much it is," Clem said. " But angels from Heaven couldn't sell peaches for anything on a market like this. You know, Katti, I've been thinking maybe that freeze was a blessing in disguise to us. I'm beginning to believe it was."

It wasn't irrelevant. Clem had been pounding his typewriter steadily ever since we had been on the island. I could follow the groove his mind worked in when he went on.

" You haven't read Smoky Seas yet either. That story is going to sell. I've got an idea for another one afterwards, too."

We stayed on. We swam — we fished for whiting in the surf — we went crabbing in the creek — we lay

(220)

on the beach in the warm evenings and watched the yellow moon swing up out of Africa. I learned how to say " money, money, money " before the shooting stars disappeared.

Once on a bright night we watched an enormous sea turtle crawl out of the ocean, a splendid powerful sea monster glistening with phosphorous.

There was a night too when we caught the tail end of a West Indian hurricane, when the house creaked and groaned, and the heavy shutters crashed. The moon rose half hidden by a flying cloud. Clem and I fought our way to the beach and watched the great seas pound up and shatter themselves against the dunes. A ghost crab scuttling to his hole was lifted by the wind and whirled a dozen feet away, bracing himself in a sort of fantastically absurd dance.

A little sand strip of an island, a covey of old, carefully built houses, squatting behind a barricade of dunes. White-wash peeling away. Scrubby trees beaten low by the sea winds. White herons, with long green legs, fishing patiently in the salt creek. Cardinals nesting. Painted buntings and humming birds pecking at flaming oleander bushes. Trickle of flowing wells. The incessant boom and hiss of the surf on the hard packed narrow beach. Never a ship on the ocean except the dories of the darky deep-sea fishermen, who go out before day over the curve of the world to supply the island

(221)

with fish, and come see-sawing in through the surf at sundown.

Primitive, clean as the sea itself, unspoiled. Forty miles of really terrible road and the lack of a ferry across a wide river had kept it an ideal island.

22

September is a bad time to come back to the Sandhills. The orchard was losing its leaves. They were blowing about, parched and yellowing. Ragged weeds had sprung up since the last cultivation.

" Something really has to be done about the floor joists," I remember saying the first thing when I went into the house.

The floor boards were creaking under my feet at every step. A too friendly little snake, about ten inches long, was in the act of crawling under a French door. There was dust and heat and the same old dry wind. But the pines smelt delicious and the shrubs and little trees we had planted about the house had grown. A trellis on the terrace was covered with long-stemmed orange-yellow roses. When I had picked a bowl full and opened the windows the whole living room had a different atmosphere. After all this was really home.

I was sitting on the floor unpacking suitcases when Mimi came in. She had a quite new, blind kitten to drop in my lap. I had to sit very still while she got the others. They held their little paws folded in, and mewed and protested weakly as she half dragged, half carried them. Mimi rubbed against me, her bobbed tail held straight up in the air. She purred loudly even when I lifted and squeezed her big seven-toed paws. The kittens had long tails but had extra toes too, like their mother. Their feet looked as though they wore mittens.

Warren said, " I'm sure Mimi's children are all boys this time. Clem won't have to kill any of them."

" I won't quench that youthful optimism," I thought, but I knew how it would be. Already the weary routine of the farm had begun.

We drove over to Samarcand for the mail that evening. We passed Old Man Britt, trudging over on foot, and picked him up.

" What's the news, Amos? "

" Tain't much happened since you been gone, ma'm. Did you hear 'bout the shootin'? "

" No, what shooting? "

" Why, they shot up Herb MacCoy's house. Shot through his doors and windows, shot through his roof."

" Anybody hurt? "

" No, I reckon Herb must have been layin' on the floor or somethin'."

" Who did it? "

" Well, I don't rightly know. Seems like it must have been Tom Brady." (One of the wild youngsters in the neighborhood.)

" But why was Tom shooting at Herb? "

" Why, he was kinda annoyed with Herb."

" What was he annoyed about? "

" Well, Herb was shootin' at him."

I was sure now I really was home again. Back in the Sandhills where men are literal.

Rory gave notice he was leaving.

" I don't aim to trade for another year, Mr. Ripley," he said. " T'aint that I don't like it here, but Janie she's a-fussin' to live in town and we're goin' to try the mill at Biscoe. You'll find everything in fine shape."

We were neither glad nor sorry to have Rory go. He had been a negative soul, neither too good nor too bad. Once again we considered Old Man Britt and discarded the idea on account of his bad boys. The oldest one, Clyde, was doing a hitch in the Marines at present, pushed to it by the threat of a reform school if he didn't clear out of the neighborhood. There were always tales about the younger one — selling his pa's hens and drinkin' up the cash. Runnin' off with a twelve-year-old girl in the next county and marryin' her when her daddy went gunnin' for him — poisonin' a neighbor's hunting

(225)

dog — and so on and on. They were pleasant mannered, agreeable boys, too.

We had various applicants. In the end we engaged Thomas. He was a tall, well built young fellow, dressed in a leather golf jacket and white duck trousers. There was nothing rural about him at first glance. He might have been one of the drug store sheiks from Aberdeen or Southern Pines. As a matter of fact that was his ambition. He had been born a farm boy, tried being a butcher's assistant in a small town, and, losing his job, had been forced to drift back to farming.

He was a new broom that swept very clean. In the first few days after he and his ineffectual little wife and their two children moved over he made things hum. He straightened up the barn and packhouse, re-sorted and re-stacked the left-over crates, and generally slicked up the place. He had a quiet, respectful manner, and gave the impression of being decidedly a cut above the average.

He had been with us a couple of weeks when I heard him beating his little girl. It was late afternoon. I was in the garden and the wind was blowing from the direction of their house. I could hear little Pearl's screams, the sympathetic wails of the two little boys and the heavy smack, smack of a hand against flesh.

"Oh, fer God's sake, Rafe, leave her be!" It was Mrs. Thomas' high-pitched, frightened whine.

There was no answer but the children's cries and the intermittent blows.

It got on my nerves. I went in the house and told Clem.

"But after all, Katti," he said, "they are his children. They may need a good whipping. It's up to him."

That was perfectly reasonable. I walked up the road away from the noise. I still felt something ought to be done but I didn't know just what.

Old Sarah said next day, " Mr. Thomas was feeling mighty good las' night. That po' li'l Pearl's got her backside black an' blue today."

" Say what you mean, Sarah. Had Thomas been drinking? "

" Well, I couldn't rightfully say, ma'm. I don't know for certain." (No darky ever tells a direct fact discreditable to a white man.) " But he sure has him a natural high temper if he ain't been."

" What had Pearl done, Sarah? "

"Her? Why she was playin' and breshed against him, I heered, and knocked the cup outta his han'. I reckon' he wasn't a-holdin' it none too steady."

I went to Clem again.

" His work's done all right," Clem said. " He was on the job at sunup this morning. I tell you, Katti, as long as a man does his work you have no complaint,

(227)

even if it isn't pleasant to have him whip his children where you can hear him."

" But drunk? " I insisted.

" Old Sarah's nonsense. They all drink." Clem dismissed the subject.

I tried to forget it, too. But there's this difference between the country and town. In town if such a thing as a man beating his children, as you consider too hard, should come to your attention, you can say to yourself, " Oh, well, there are agencies to take care of such cases. If it gets too bad someone, the policeman on the beat probably, will report it." You can shift the responsibility. But out in the country where the man is your employee it is your responsibility. It is for you to decide whether he is beating his child too severely or not, and if anything is done about it you are the one who must do it.

It happened again more than once while the Thomases stayed. I used to walk up the road, and distance would drown the sound of little Pearl's cries, or I would shut the windows on that side of the house, or sing or talk loudly to shut out the noise of the blows and the children's screams. As long as Thomas did his day's work we let him handle his family affairs as he liked. We were probably wrong. But unless a man actually commits a crime and injures someone, so that you can call the sheriff and have him arrested, what can you do? We

(228)

could have dismissed him, but that would not have helped the situation. It would have been a relief for me not to have to know about his cruelty, but it wouldn't have stopped him abusing his family.

I found I had to think out questions for myself that in town one can dodge. I didn't do anything to make the world a better place. I just compromised by saying to myself, " Oh, well, it's none of my business after all." But I had to do what in town I could have avoided. I had to look at myself squarely and decide whether or not I was one of those willing to become my brother's keeper. I found I was not.

Just on our little farm and within a few miles of it there was enough social welfare work needing to be done to have kept one woman busy a whole lifetime. Ignorance of simple hygiene — sickness caused by lack of knowledge and neglect — children undernourished and anæmic because their mothers didn't cook their food properly and their fathers didn't bother to grow an adequate garden — to cite a few lesser evils. I, or anyone else, could have spent a full day, three hundred and sixty-five days a year, helping and teaching these people.

This, of course, is just as true of most towns as it is of rural districts. The difference is this: in the city you can fool yourself by looking the other way and by believing that the welfare agents have it all in hand. On

(229)

your own farm you can do as much or as little as you, yourself, wish. But you cannot blind yourself to the facts.

I knew old Amos pulled his own teeth with wire pliers to save a dollar's dentist bill — " since Clyde, who useta do my tooth pullin', joined the Marines." I knew an old woman near us whose brother-in-law tried to remove a cataract from her eye with a farrier's knife. I knew that in this age of medical science Amos' " Old Aunt Dilly, a powerful old doctor woman," still brewed teas of herbs to cure anything from cancer to whooping cough.

But we let the people about us struggle with their own aches and pains and cures and their own way of life and we borrowed money from the bank and applied it on our orchard.

Thomas hated horses and mules. " How can a man plough an orchard right, the way it had oughta be ploughed, 'less he's got him a tractor, Mr. Ripley? Over to the Bell Hiley, where I been workin', they wouldn't have no horse ploughin' there."

And more and more, and day after day, until Clem, too, was convinced that Thomas knew what he was talking about and that we did need to equip the farm with a tractor.

The magic phrase — " A modern farm equipped with machinery."

(230)

Thomas knew of the very tractor for us. It was an almost new Fordson. Its owner had bought it and used it only a few times. Each time he took it out something went wrong and it had to go to the local garage. The garage man was a friend of Thomas'.

"Mr. Ripley, Mr. Martin got plum tired of payin' repair bills on that tractor. He sold it cheap to Sam" (the garage man) "and Sam found out then what the trouble was. 'Twas just the crank case was out o' line. They put it together wrong at the factory. Sam's got it all jake now and you kin buy it cheap."

The upshot of it was we did buy it for two hundred dollars. Thomas was right. It was as good as a new tractor, a bargain. It pleased him very much for a while and he cultivated the orchard clean that fall. We sold the horses and as we had no cow now there was no stock for him to have to worry with through the winter — which pleased him, too. We realized we should have to buy horses in summer to haul the peach wagons and do other jobs the tractor couldn't. We knew we'd pay more for horses, too, in the spring, but we hoped we'd save more than enough on what they'd eat during the winter to offset the extra cost, and in the course of years make this saving pay for the tractor.

The tractor was a fascinating new toy. It squatted in the shed looking like some sullen prehistoric beast, but we found it very useful during that winter. We rigged

(231)

it up to run a gasoline saw and cut wood. When the stationary engine was out of order, it could pump. Thomas was a fair mechanic and young Rob Britt, now fifteen years old, became his shadow, holding wrenches, crawling beneath the great monster to grease it, or just standing in deferential awe looking at it.

23

Milton Bird and Clem were starting a tutoring school. The tutoring they had done during last season had advertised them and they had enough pupils to warrant renting an apartment to teach in this year. It meant Clem would spend his days in Pinehurst through the winter. Thomas with the help of Old Man Britt, young Rob and possibly a darky or so, could do the pruning and other winter work.

"Oh, yes," Clem said, in answer to my question. "They'll do it slower than with me there, but even if it takes an extra hand my time is worth more than a two dollar a day darky's is. Thomas knows how it ought to be done and I'll inspect, of course.

Helen Bird and I offered our services to help in the school if they got any very little fellows and needed us. Until Christmas it was a dull winter. The long drive in the open car to Pinehurst in the morning, the unappetizing luncheon at the Greek restaurant, snatched between pupils, the long drive home in the late afternoon. And the hours between, long hours of teaching. How friendly and comforting the firelight used to look from the windows of our house in the twilight!

" It isn't really so bad, Katti," Clem used to say. " It's dull, of course, but I'll make between fifteen hundred and two thousand dollars out of it, and we have to live."

So it had come to that, I thought to myself. A make-shift job with no future to it. A tide over to what?

We were not even having the advantages of country life. All day long we were away from the farm shut up in an apartment teaching school. Clem was busy with his pupils usually until six in the afternoon and oftentimes Saturday, too. Always the farm was on our minds. Was Thomas shirking? Was he watching young Rob and seeing that he didn't steal the truck to joy ride? Was he remembering to hoe the grass away from the roots of the lower block of Belles before he put the fertilizer out? Nights and Sundays Clem wrote and I stayed indoors and caught up with housekeeping. Without me old Sarah was a rudderless ship.

For a couple of years there had been gossipy rumors in the fall that someone or other wasn't coming home this winter. They always proved true.

This fall I said to Clem, " You don't believe it about the Derbys not coming back though, do you, Clem? "

" Well, I don't know. I don't quite see how he can leave as big a proposition as his orchard. Still . . ."

I tried to believe it wasn't so, but when the Derbys came down in October they confirmed the rumor. They were back only to pack their things.

Roger said, " It's the life of a rabbit living in New York. Diving in and out of holes in the ground. I can't tell you how I miss the Sandhills." But there was a lack of sincerity in his voice and the worried frown had gone from between his eyes.

Roger was going into investment banking.

The Pumpellys were already gone. The Tuckermans had gone back to Boston. Various others left. We hoped it was only temporary — that our neighbors would come back. I think they rather expected to themselves. " They'll all come back," I kept saying to myself, " when peaches begin to pay again."

There began to be sprinkled over the section, not deserted orchards, but deserted houses. Big comfortable houses of people who had gone away to make a living. The trees were kept up, but the owners' houses stood lonely and untenanted, pathetic monuments to a dream that hadn't come true.

Of those who stayed, one after another went into some side line to support his orchard through the lean

(235)

years. As Ralph Page put it, " We'll have to learn to live off of the tourists now."

Liv Biddle opened a real estate office in Pinehurst. Frank Dudgeon became postmaster. Billy Cowgill started a cotton mill. Harry Waring was already selling fertilizer, and Charlie Mason had some time before gone into real estate and insurance. I could go on practically through the list of Northern peach growers.

The difference was particularly noticeable at parties that winter. Where there had been peach growers with a sprinkling of resort people, we began to find resort people and a few peach growers. We were no longer a composite group with the same interests and aims. There was very little talk of growing peaches and farming any more. Everyone had his own individual business now, and talking shop was frowned on just as in a similar group in town.

I knew of only one grower who was well ahead of the peach game. This one was John Galsworthy's fictional character, Jon Forsyte. Mr. Galsworthy had visited the Sandhills during the boom. In the current Forsyte novel (I think it was " The White Monkey ") Jon made a fortune in Sandhill peaches. We did think of organizing a Jon Forsyte Club, but nobody had the heart. Losing steadily, with a darkening future, was too serious to most people to joke about.

Clem had more faith in his writing than I had. He

(236)

worked hard at the school, but he was convinced that writing was his side line.

Every morning on our way over to Pinehurst, and every evening on our way home, we stopped at Samarcand for the mail. Clem had two manuscripts out, a serial, " Smoky Seas," that he had written at the shore last summer and a short story. They had both been out and returned several times and sent on their travels again. We dreaded seeing large, square, manilla envelopes, but we raced frantically through the ordinary letters, searching for acceptances.

It had been so long since Clem had sold a story that it was more a kind of game than anything else to me to plan in daydreams what we'd do with the money if one actually did sell again. Hope dies hard. If one did, it might bring in as much as three hundred dollars.

And then, in Christmas week, there were a flock of letters in one mail. The first few were the usual stuff. There were several bills. There was a franked out bulletin from the Farm Bureau, addressed to Mr. Elements Ripley (an excellent name incidentally, for a farmer). There was a chatty little note from a concern that put out trailers for carrying polo ponies, who were sure a trailer for carrying his ponies would prove a constant pleasure to Captain Glemens Ripley, if he'd only be persuaded to try one. But the last two letters, at the bottom of the pile, we recognized without opening, by the addresses

(237)

in the corners. They were from the magazines reading Clem's stories.

" Let me open them for luck," I said.

Clem tried to grab them, but I held them tight and ran out to the car.

Old Man Britt was waiting. " Miz Ripley, reckon Cap'll give me a ride home? "

" Climb in," I told him.

I opened one letter. While I was reading it, Clem grabbed the other and tore off the envelope. " They're going to pay me four hundred dollars for that short story. Good God! " he gasped.

I said, " Clem, they've taken " Smoky Seas " and they've paid for it. Here's a check." I hesitated. I held the check out of the car window at arm's length. I tried to look worried. " Clem," I said, " it's for only — only — " I had to giggle. " Clem," I said, " it's for sixteen hundred dollars."

Clem said, " Let me see it quick."

Old Man Britt said, " What, you mean somebody's payin' Cap sixteen hundred dollars for just writing a story — and it 'tain't nothing but a pack of lies neither? I can't see what gets into some folks. Better see if the check's good, Cap."

We felt absurdly rich. We felt reckless. We felt as though a millstone, the millstone of a drab, colorless future, had been lifted from our necks.

"And think of all the stories you've got in your head, Clem," I said. "You and the encyclopedia ought to be able to keep right on turning them out."

It was a great Christmas week. We drove up to Greensboro and bought some clothes. Clem got a new overcoat. We bought toys for Warren and the Thomas children, and the little Sanderses. This year we didn't have to eke out the stockings for the servants and the farm people with nuts and apples. We had a regular orgy of buying; true a large part of it was at the ten cent store but it was an orgy just the same.

"I didn't count shooting stars for nothing, Clem," I said.

Everybody had a present, even Mimi. A red collar with a bell, which she had to wear Christmas day and hated, just as most men hate their Christmas neckties.

"It's the turning of the tide," I thought. "Money from the tutoring school coming in, money from the stories — there'll be more stories and more money. But everything goes in threes — Money, money, money, I counted on the stars; maybe in spite of everything there'll be money from the orchard this year."

Years before, Clem's first check for a story had seemed easy money. Rejection slip after rejection slip had shown us it was not as easy as it looked, but it was different this time. Clem had been writing and studying writing now for years. The work he had put in was beginning to show a return at last. Peaches were his real business, but writing was the only side line we had tried so far that had showed a real profit.

Clem said, "If the damn orchard will only take care of itself through these years of overproduction, I believe I can at least make enough out of writing for us to live on."

Hours of tutoring other people's children hurry by!

Endless questioning of Thomas, and endless inspection of farm work, hurry by!

Sleet and wind and rain and cold weather, hurry by!

Let the days come when Clem can write in peace, when he doesn't have to keep one eye on the fire to see that it doesn't die down, when the children have all gone North, when Thomas and the men are working within sight of the open window.

24

Spring!

Melithy was a colored woman, who came in occasionally when the work piled up, to help Sarah with the washing.

"Melithy, do you think you ought to bend over the tub so much?"

"Ma'm?"

"Melithy, I mean, do you think it's good for you? You are going to have a baby, aren't you?" (It was obvious that she was.)

"Well, ma'm, I don't rightly know, ma'm. But I most generally does this time of year."

Spring!

To me the blooming of the orchard always began our year. With the bursting of the buds optimism and new hope were born in us too. All the old scores we held against the trees seemed to be wiped out. It was a fresh start. There was that inevitable thrill in the spring of '27. The bright new washed freshness of the trees blooming in the clean sand.

" And what a crop there'll be this summer, Cap," said old Amos, poking his head through the door the first day it was pleasant enough to leave it open and let the sunshine flood in, " after the rest the Lord seen fitten for to give them last year."

The trees were blooming early. They were at their height the first week of March.

The seventh was a rainy day. I went to a card party in the afternoon at Pinehurst. While we were playing, somebody said, " Why, it looks just like snow. I do believe it is snowing a few flakes! But, of course they are melting as soon as they touch the ground."

" Clem," I said, when he stopped for me a few minutes later, " doesn't the weather worry you? Look at the snow."

" It isn't really cold and so long as it's just this snowy rain with a wind behind it there won't be a freeze. This little flurry of snow is a joke."

" Clem, someone just told me she remembered six inches of snow in Pinehurst one March."

" Who said that? "

I told him.

" Oh, for cat's sake, you can't believe a word she says. She gets everything wrong. Who ever heard

(242)

of six inches of snow here, at any time, let alone March? "

The big wet flakes were still mixed with rain and were still melting as soon as they touched the ground, when we reached our house.

When I woke up in the morning I knew there was something queer. There was a strange unnatural brightness and stillness. I pulled back the window curtains. The ground was dazzlingly white. The peach trees were squatty pink bushes, their lower branches partially buried. I had never seen so much snow before. With the early sun on it it was really lovely. I looked toward Clem and I felt guilty to have harbored such a thought.

Clem's teeth were set. " Talk about Providence," he said. " Freezes and hail and drought are natural. But I swear even a farmer's God is going out of his way to send snow like this at any time of the year, much less March."

It proved to be twenty-seven inches deep. We measured it with a rule in a dozen different places.

Old Sarah and Sally, the girl we had now in place of Lacy (who had grown big enough to work in the fields), were snowed into their house. We had to dig them out before we could have breakfast. It was pleasant and sunny outdoors, ideal weather for playing in the snow.

(243)

The orchard was the silliest looking thing, merrily in bloom, like somebody in white flannels and a straw hat at Christmas time. We could hardly walk in the drifts. I watched Mimi tripping blithely over the crust on her oversized, mitten-like paws. She looked back insultingly over her shoulder at Thomas' mongrel floundering behind.

Our telephone was working and we talked to Milton about the school. His voice came eerie and thin over the wires. He told us Pinehurst was paralyzed. They were trying to deliver groceries and mail on horseback. All the trains were snowed in. A man and a girl had been frozen to death at Aberdeen.

Fortunately, we had a lot of home-cured sausage and plenty of flour. We had not only to feed ourselves but to lend supplies to the Thomases and feed the improvident family of darkies who last year sharecropped the few acres of cotton, and still hung on in our little shack. I rationed out the food and prepared to enjoy the snow.

We made snow houses and ploughed about in it, but after a few hours it got tiresome. After three days, it was completely loathsome to us both. Clem was out of cigarettes and thoroughly cross. We were sick of the taste of sausage and of having no cream for our coffee in the mornings. But the really worrying thing, of course, was the blooming trees.

(244)

Clem floundered about in the orchard opening the blooms to try and discover if they had all been killed. Amazingly all he opened were alive.

But I was afraid to bolster myself up with false hope. I couldn't believe it wasn't just chance that he had happened on live buds. I wouldn't even go in the orchard.

By Saturday we had been snowed in about five days. Darthea and Bill Cowgill were having a treasure hunt and telephoned us to come over. We were sick to death of being prisoners. Forced to stay on the farm and be surrounded by the trees still in full bloom in the melting snow, made me feel the way I think a bird dog must who has a chicken he killed tied around his neck. I knew we weren't to blame but I somehow felt guilty.

The snow was still too deep for the car to get through but Rob Britt, ever ingenious, got an old buggy at his father's house and made a set of rope harness for it. The highway was open and Ellen and Stuart Maurice would meet us there in their car.

It took us an hour and a half to drive to Samarcand, what with the harness breaking and one thing and another, but we met the Maurices and were at the Country Club, where the hunt started, on time. It was the most fun of any treasure hunt I ever went on — not that either Clem or I found the treasure, but we looked across the room at each other when the turkey came in for supper. We were both thinking the same thought, " Thank God it isn't sausage."

As long as the snow lasted and we had it to contend with as an immediate and present problem it had kept my mind somewhat from dwelling on what I supposed would mean the loss of yet another crop. When it melted, and things dropped back into their routine, it was I who couldn't bear to look out of the windows and see the orchard. Clem kept his faith that the buds were not killed.

One morning, while I was dressing for school, Clem came up from the barn where he'd been to give Thomas some directions. He was wearing a broad grin. He had his hands behind his back.

" Which one do you want? " he said.

" Both," I said.

He held them out. They were full of infinitely minute, but unmistakable peaches.

" So you were right and they weren't frozen," I gasped.

" Just enough to save thinning," he said. "We're going to have a big crop, and they say Georgia really *is* frozen out this year."

"That's what they say every year, Clem," I said.

But we couldn't help but feel optimistic. Surely the crop had not weathered that terrific snow just to ma-

(246)

ture, be packed and shipped, and then dumped ig-
nominiously in the North River as we had heard so
many carloads were last year.

As the spring gave way to summer there were more
and more rumors from Georgia. "It's hard on those
fellows down there," we said, "but it's an ill wind
that blows nobody any good, and if we all had a crop
we'd all lose money."

The Sandhills crop was short, too. Lots of orchards
had been hard hit by the snow.

Our peaches were almost twice as big as golf balls
when Clem and I, driving home from somewhere one
afternoon, turned out of the road to let a car going the
other way pass by. The car slowed up and came to a
full stop.

The driver of it proved to be a friend of ours, one of
the shrewdest peach men in the business. He had an interest in, or handled, at a guess perhaps a fourth of
the fruit in the section now that peaches had not paid
for several years and many Northern growers had either
sold their orchards outright or else mortgaged them to
the hilt.

"Clem," he called, sticking his head out of the
car window, "I've been over looking at your fruit.
It looks good and I'll buy it from you if you like?"

Now yesterday — last week — this morning — a
moment ago, both Clem and I would have jumped at

(247)

the chance of selling this crop outright if we could come even on the year's expenses. Except for the familiar rumor that Georgia was frozen out (that hardy perennial, which had always been disproved when the season rolled around and Georgia shipped more cars than ever) as far as we knew we had no real reason to expect anything but a cash loss this year. But now that our friend was about to make us an offer, I began to feel a perverse hesitation.

" How much will you give me? " Clem asked.

" A dollar and a quarter for Belles and a dollar and seventy-five for Elbertas."

I jumped. Clem says I pinched him hard.

" I'll think it over," Clem was saying slowly, " and let you know."

" Decide by tonight, then. I'll tell you how it is. I've sold the fruit at those prices on one of the orchards I'm handling." He named the orchard. " The buyers want Elbertas. You've got three-fourths Elbertas, I understand. I'm letting you in on it, because I need your extra Elbertas. All you have to do is deliver them packed on the platform in the village. Think it over and telephone me." He threw in the clutch.

We waved good-bye. Clem said, " He's selling his fruit for that and he's a shrewd peach man." But his tone lacked conviction.

" Ye-es," I said. " But the buyers? They must think

(248)

the price is going up. They're probably big jobbers and they may be in a position to know."

" Perhaps, but they may be wrong. If Georgia comes in with a big crop it will knock the bottom out of the market the way it did last year."

I said, " That's true."

We drove along for half a mile without speaking. I think each of us knew what the other was thinking. I know it didn't surprise me when Clem said at last —

" We've gambled on this thing for six years. For four years we didn't have any production. The last two years we took a beating. If this should turn out to be a big year and I got cold feet and sold now to do a little better than break even, I'd kick myself the rest of my life."

I said, " Yes, and the people who are buying that fruit think it's going up. You know what Ned Beall used to say about poker, ' raise or quit, don't call.' "

Clem said, " And yet an hour ago I'd have let any-one have it at that price and tickled to do it."

I laughed. "Clem," I said, "Do you remember that old woman in the clay I told you about, the time I was trying to buy her walnut chest? ' If you want hit, I want hit.' "

That night Clem telephoned and turned down the of-fer. The minute we heard the clicking of the receiver as he hung up we both of us had a change of heart.

(249)

" Do you think we've made a mistake? " I asked.

Clem frowned miserably. " How in hell do I know? It's too late now. I don't know. I suppose I should have talked it over with some of the growers before I decided. I wish I'd telegraphed Roger. Anyway we're in for shipping the crop ourselves now."

25

"We'll be on the safe side and ship this crop on the cheap," Clem said. "We won't fool with crates, but bushel the fruit."

"And I'll be packhouse boss, and use the local labor," I said, "and we'll save the price of Georgia professionals. Oh, Clem, maybe we're going to make some money at last."

"God, I hope so. And I hope I don't kick myself for not selling when I had the chance."

The tutoring school had closed. Clem had sixteen hundred dollars coming to him. He bought our bushel baskets and engaged the labor for the crop.

Amos was right and it would be a big crop. Weather conditions were pretty good and the peaches were swelling fast. Nobody we talked to had any real information about the Georgia crop but the general feeling was one of optimism.

" I guess we did the right thing, Katti," Clem said.

" Sure, we had to take the chance. You can't lose for two years and then not gamble on getting it back your third. That's farming."

One day as we drove back from Samarcand, just before the crop began, we passed a tall broad-shouldered youth walking. We slowed down and as is usual on country roads offered him a lift. When the boy turned I noticed something vaguely familiar about him.

" How you, Cap? " he said, with a pleasant grin.

" Why it's Clyde Britt, isn't it? " I said.

" It sure is, Miz Ripley, back from the Marines. Been to Quantico. Been to Nicaragua. Been all over everywheres and back to God's country."

" Going to stay here now, Clyde, or going to try another hitch? " Clem asked.

" Stay if I can git me a job, I reckon. Can I work for you through the crop, Cap? "

Clem looked doubtful.

" Clyde," I said, " how would you like to work for me? I can use you in the packhouse."

" With all them good looking girls? " Clyde asked gleefully.

Clem looked still more doubtful.

" You would do it," he said when we dropped Clyde at the crossroads. " If he wrecks the packhouse and the girls all quit in the middle of the season you've got nobody but yourself to blame."

I looked back and saw Clyde's lean figure disappearing up the road. I said, " It takes a boy above the average in intelligence to be the worst boy in the neighborhood anyhow."

A day or two later I asked Clem who he had decided on to drive the truck. He looked a little sheepish.

" Rob Britt," he said.

We both laughed. We had held off having old Amos on the place in spite of the fact that he was an excellent farmer, on account of his two bad boys and now I had hired one and Clem the other.

" Young Rob will be driving the truck where I can watch him," Clem said.

Rob was a splendid hand with any kind of machinery. He had a good head on his square shoulders, too. This winter he'd been too busy to work, but he'd lived pretty well with his father and he'd enjoyed many of the luxuries of life.

Young Rob had had five dollars in the world in the fall. He had paid this down as the first installment on a victrola. Sarah and Warren had been over to hear it and they said it made fine loud music. But young Rob, after a few weeks, tired of anything so tame as an instrument that played just what you told it to. He hankered for the thrill and uncertainty of a radio.

(253)

He had no money but he solved this small difficulty by turning in the victrola as a down payment on the radio.

After a time this new toy palled and he turned in the radio in a different village as the first installment on a second-hand Ford. He was contented at last. He loved the Ford.

I don't know how he handled the installment companies that had let him have the victrola and the radio, but when the dealer came over to take back the Ford after several weeks when no further payments had been forthcoming, Rob wrecked the car. It was already pretty decrepit when he got it. He took out enough parts so that the dealer couldn't get it home without a towing. It looked as though it would never run again.

The dealer must have decided that it wasn't worth hauling back to the garage. He left it, probably with a faint hope that if he did Rob might eventually be made to pay a little something more on it.

Rob had the decency to wait a few days before he fixed it up so that it ran like a charm.

Driving the truck was not work but play to young Rob, except as it might prove irksome to have to do it at the times other people told him to instead of at his leisure. But he wanted money to buy gasoline for his Ford, so he was delighted to get the job.

(254)

It was soon time to begin thinking of getting the rest of the labor together. Our season this year began about the middle of July.

The report of good prices to come was still floating about. Everything — the short crop which was now evident throughout the country, and the good quality of our own fruit — pointed to our making a profit.

"It looks now," Clem said, "like just about what we were offered: a dollar and a quarter for Belles and a dollar seventy-five for Elbertas. I'm glad just the same that I held off. It may be better."

Even the American Growers, usually cadgy, were caught in the prevailing optimism. "Yes," they said, "the market's up. If it'll just hold when the heavy shipments begin."

I was as excited as though I held thirteen spades.

When the Georgia Belles were ready to come, Clem went out with the pickers, and I took over the packhouse alone.

We were busheling with a home-made grading machine, worked by gravity. It was built so that the peaches poured down an inclined plane, where the girls could pick out the culls as they rolled past. Many of the big orchards had found peach grading machinery unsatisfactory, and, for busheling, which is a very much simpler pack than crates, were using these gravity tables.

We estimated six times as big a crop this year as

(255)

our first year. Our packhouse was a very different place from what it had been that season when Minnie, Cherry and I had packed the crop. It was more like a small factory now.

My job as packhouse foreman was to keep things running smoothly, to make sure that everyone did his own work, to see that a slow grader or ringer did not check the constant flow of fruit, or that a slow busheler did not let the table get choked up. I had to keep the man who poured the peaches from the picking boxes into the gravity table going. I had to frown at Clyde Britt when he shocked the girls by undoing his shirt to show the tatooed mermaid on his chest. I had to keep Warren, who had begged for a job, from getting underfoot. I had to inspect the finished packages. I had to be sure that the labels were all on straight. I had to check the loads on to the truck. I had to dicker with cull buyers. In short the packhouse boss must watch each little thing, lend a hand where it is needed, and see that the whole thing clicks precisely as it should.

After our first shipment of Belles we knew we had been right in not selling ahead of time. At the start of our Belles, the American Growers could sell the cars for a dollar and a half — a day later a dollar sixty — a dollar eighty-five — and going up. The buyers began clamoring for peaches.

I heard an old peach man say, " I reckon we was

right in the Sandhills. Those fellows down in north Georgia planted their orchards on too high land."

"Sure did," a packer said who had come up that way. "Ain't a peach there this year."

Now that I knew peaches were paying, I didn't care how hard I worked. I could be up at daylight, take only fifteen minutes out for luncheon, work over accounts and manifest sheets 'til late at night, be back on the job at daylight, and all the time my heart was singing. To be making a profit at last! To be getting real money for our fruit! It was what we had been looking forward to for six years.

We were shipping into a rising market. The first carload we shipped, our own car, every bushel our own Belles of Georgia, sold f.o.b. for a dollar and eighty-five cents. To think a little over a month ago we would have sold the whole crop gladly for a dollar twenty-five.

"If we can get a dollar eighty-five for Belles," Clem said, "Elbertas ought to bring two dollars."

We really thought they'd bring more but we were afraid to say it in words. A feeling that if we spoke out loud that farmer God of the crops might hear us and playfully send some unforeseen disaster.

The first few days we were busy getting the pickers and packers licked into shape. They were mostly men and girls from isolated clay farms. The men pick and the girls pack. They come in family groups for the

(257)

most part. They look on the peach season as the big holiday of their year, the next best thing to a revival. It's different from the routine of their farm work. They work in gangs. They eat quantities of soft peaches. The men fight among themselves and make love to the girls. It's all a frolic to them. The peach season is only serious to the owner. You must humor, you must coax, you must make concessions. You must always remember that these people are absolutely necessary to you and that if they are rubbed the wrong way they are entirely capable of simply walking off.

The first day of the Elbertas Art, the bushel topper, went on a drunk. He was noisily drunk. He sang as he worked. He used language that shocked the girls.

Things reached the point where I had to tell Clyde Britt to take him off. There was a minute when a battle seemed inevitable. Art doubled his heavy fist, but he let it drop. He was sagging drunk by now. The minute passed. Incidentally that night he attacked his wife with an axe and spent a month in jail in consequence.

Clyde took over his job, but he was untrained and the baskets piled up still untopped. A drizzle of rain saved us. The pickers had to stop work for an hour and Clyde caught up with the grading table.

I'd been good and worried. If those peaches had spoiled through standing overnight in the packhouse it would have been disastrous. Two dollars a bushel for

(258)

Elbertas. The American Growers assured us they could get that much now. And that meant better than eight hundred dollars a car.

There was the slack Tuesday forenoon I watched Thomas following the gang of pickers. It was a colored crew we had borrowed from Samarcand.

Thomas yelled, " Git 'em off boys — they gotta come. Hey there, black boy! Step out. Hurry up — move along — git along there."

He had been drinking and he rolled a little as he sought footing in the loose sand.

A couple, a light yellow girl in a short frock, and a lithe black boy kept well ahead of the others. They laughed, their heads close together as they picked from the same trees.

An hour afterward, Thomas was reporting to Clem at lunch time. " By God, Mr. Ripley, I seen them black devils gittin' ahead of the crowd. I'm pretty slippy myself when it comes to keepin' niggers on the job, an' I caught them two in a peach tree together. I 'most stepped on his legs. They jumped I'll say — ' you black so and so ' — I hollered at them. She just flouted her head at me and went to work. Would you believe it, Mr. Ripley, when I happened to turn around and look back at her she was just a-snappin' off the peaches and throwin' 'em on the ground behind my back."

(259)

Next season the same girl picked for us, holding a three-months-old baby in the crook of her arm. Thomas was revenged if he had known it.

Wednesday we had another Elberta car. It was a big season for us, a season of hard work for everyone, but especially for Clem and me. But who cared? The cars were rolling out and the money was rolling in. By the end of the first week we had made our year's expenses. From then on everything was velvet.

After the first few days, the packhouse crew settled down to a steady routine. One of the best men in the picking gang came up to top bushels and soon learned to top faster than Art had. We had worried some about Clyde Britt, Amos' bad boy whom we had picked up on the road that morning. But we needn't have. Whatever may have been wrong with Clyde's morals, and from what the neighbors said there would seem to have been plenty, there was nothing wrong with his head. I began to find that I could leave things to him. As the season went on he became sort of appendage to me. He ran errands. He traded with cull buyers. In an harrassed moment one day, I even turned the cash box over to him. Later I threw caution to the winds, and he became its custodian — sometimes with well over a hundred dollars in it. He helped load the truck and learned to check the loads. In short he lent a hand wherever it was needed most, and did without being

(260)

told anything which in an emergency might be required of a packhouse boss, and which I, as a woman, hadn't the physical strength to do, or for any reason hadn't the time.

All day long through the season the cull buyers drove up in cars and trucks. The men who wanted sixty bushels to resell and the men who wanted one to take home "for cannin' purposes." Long lean fellows in overalls who "didn't come fer to buy no peaches this time. Just come to look 'round and eat a few." The woman in a straw hat with a wreath of faded rose buds who kept me fidgeting with impatience, as the packhouse work went slack, while she told me her grandma's receipt for peach jam. The man who wanted a special bushel, packed a certain way of his own, to ship to a friend. But there was a compensation. Even culls were bringing anywhere from fifty cents to a dollar and a quarter a bushel.

The tin roof crackled with the heat. The peaches flowed down the grading table all day long in a never ending stream. The graders complained that their eyes hurt, and some of them even got seasick. The men sweated at the turntable, at stacking baskets, at loading the truck. Even with three sides open to the air the shed reeked with sweat and peaches. Fuzz prickled. Gnats stung.

But every bushel neatly labeled and checked on to

(261)

the truck was bringing first a dollar eighty-five, then two dollars, then two dollars and a quarter.

" They're coming fine," The American Growers' inspector told us. " We'll try and get you two fifty next week."

It rained Saturday morning.

" Miz Ripley, you wouldn't pack Sunday, would you, ma'm? " from the girl graders.

Old Amos to the packhouse at large, " Cap Ripley believes what the Good Book says 'bout pullin' out your ox or your ass on the Sabbath Day. Ain't that right? "

The doubt on the girls' faces. " They preached against picking peaches on Sunday at the revival — they say that's how come the crop didn't bring no price last year."

Try and persuade them, Amos!

Clyde, a loyal voice crying in the wilderness, " Sure we'll help Cap out. They never stopped the war for no Sunday."

Religious argument whirled through the packhouse. Texts beat against the tin roof. Before we were aware of it the rain slacked, the sky cleared. " We'll finish up today after all, girls."

Another crisis avoided. Thank you, Amos! Thank you, Clyde! Thank you, God!

The weather stayed fair throughout the crop. The labor flirted and fought and drank, but it stuck, and we got the fruit picked and packed and in the cars by the time they were ready to roll.

And all through the ten days we picked the market climbed steadily. We felt like King Midas. Everything we had touched in the past year, Clem's stories, the tutoring school and now the peach crop, had turned to gold.

" Well this is something like it," Clem said. " We'll go on a real trip. We'll go first to New York and we'll spend the rest of the summer in New England and Canada."

The orchard lay about the house, stripped and bare. Thomas, Sam, Amos and Clyde picked up the peaches that had fallen on the ground. The packhouse was swept and clean. The picking boxes were piled tidily under shelter.

We can go away, I thought, or we can stay and have the floor joists fixed and build that new room we used to plan, or put in an electric light plant. But we didn't want to stay a day longer than was necessary. We didn't want to bother with those things. Were we cut out for farmers, I wondered. Or do all farmers feel like this? Certainly whenever we get a little money our first idea is to leave the farm. We'll be glad to come back though, I thought. For at last the system of living we were looking for is working out. The farm has declared a dividend.

(263)

We gave bonuses to our regular hands.

"What are you going to do with yours, Thomas?"

"Well I reckon I'll take me a little fishin' trip down to the seashore if Cap'll give me a few days off now the work's slack."

"Going to take Mrs. Thomas and the children along?"

"I reckon not."

I knew what Thomas' trip would be.

Old Amos said, "I reckon I'll git me a wagon, ma'm."

"But you've got a pretty good wagon already, haven't you Amos?"

"So so," Amos said. "But I've been kinda fussin' after one I seed up at Star. It's got red wheels and trim, and built of solid hickory plum through. I'm goin' to git me that wagon. It cost twenty dollars down for the first payment. And I'm goin' hitch up the old mule and get me a fruit jar of good likker and go ridin' somewheres."

The new wagon was to Amos what a good car would be to us. The old wagon perhaps corresponded to a reliable Ford or Chevrolet, but Amos wanted to go into the Buick class. Plenty of drink and something snappy to ride in. Not so different from many a broker on his vacation.

We dressed and had a round of cocktails before dinner and planned our holiday. Two months away from the farm.

A few days later, without cocktails, we looked at '27's crop from a different angle. We knew, as everyone in the section did, that it was a pure fluke. Our Georgia competitors had happened to be frozen out. We could hardly hope for that to happen two years in succession. Overproduction was still with us.

We had cleared forty-four hundred dollars. Of course, this was without deducting overhead or interest on the investment. But if you go deducting things like that you couldn't have any fun at all farming.

But if we had any doubts of the season having been a fluke, offering our farm for sale, orchard, house, farm machinery and live stock, for fifteen thousand dollars cash, convinced us of its truth. We got not even a nibble. The peach growers were not fooled by the good prices in '27. Everyone was trying to sell his orchard and no one seemed to care to pick up anybody else's even at a great bargain.

Like the insistent buzzing of a gnat in my ear, common sense and caution kept whispering, " If this year was purely a fluke, why do you go on? If your only chance is for some calamity to happen to some other orchard, aren't the odds all against you? "

But after six years of farming the gamble was in our blood. And the indisputable fact was, we had

(265)

netted forty-four hundred dollars over and above expenses this year, in spite of every prophecy and indication of an actual cash loss. All true farmers believed
in the age of miracles — to come. And if we did not
keep up our orchard all we would have would be a
pine barren farm. We had too big an investment not
to go on.

"Well, anyway, now we've made a profit I'm going to write a novel," Clem said. "It'll take nearly
a year to write, I guess, but if it catches there's a lot
more money in it than shorts."

It didn't occur to either of us that he should hesitate
to risk a year's work. We were genuinely amazed when
both Jim Boyd and Struthers Burt were dubious.

"But Clem — generally you have some idea where
you're going to sell a novel before you begin writing it."

Clem hadn't but he chucked the tutoring school and
a safe sixteen hundred dollars, and began work.

26

We had a pleasant summer in the North — the toy villages and Christmas trees of Vermont — the low blue hills and cold blue St. Lawrence that hem in Murray Bay.

When we came home in the fall we found that Thomas had become very worthless. There was nothing we could lay our hands on, but we suspected him of gypping us in a dozen petty ways. We knew he was dead-beating on the job as our bills for outside labor while we were away were much higher than they should have been. " Drunk all the time — loafin' and fightin' and beatin' up his wife and kids," the crowd around the store told us.

" My God, Mist' Ripley," Thomas said, " hit's that goddam tractor. I ride hit all day long in the dust and sand. First thing I know I'm sicker than a pup and I'm renchin' and spittin' blood."

Clem said, " Well you were the one that wanted the tractor. Anyway you don't drive it every day, so that's not the only reason you dead-beat and stay drunk."

" Aw, Mr. Ripley," Thomas said. " There ain't a damn thing to this farming for me. No money, no future. Hard work all day long. One day is just like another. You tell me not to drink, what's a man to do? "

" Well here's your chance to go back to town and look for a job," Clem told him.

" God, I couldn't make a living there neither," Thomas whined.

" Well this time it's Old Man Amos," Clem said. " Clyde will actually be an asset and the rest of us will just have to keep an eye on young Rob."

Old Amos was old fashioned and economical. He loathed the tractor from the first. The magic phrase, a modern farm equipped with machinery meant nothing to Amos.

As a matter of fact the tractor was not working out so well for us. It was more expensive to run than we had expected it to be. Of course, it could do many things that a horse couldn't do but we had to have horses or mules to pull the picking wagons during the crop, as it was impossible to be sure of renting them at that season. If we kept the horses all year they could do the farm work and we could get along without a

(268)

tractor as we had for years. It was simply a fifth wheel on our farm.

We had consoled ourselves for the extra expense with the thought that it made the work much easier for the men. A man trudging all day behind a one-horse plough is a weary sight. He has a sort of jaunty look bouncing along atop a tractor.

But old Amos would have nothing to do with it. Rob was anxious to drive it. He had tinkered with it for years. He was a little like an aviation mechanic who has served his apprenticeship in the hangar and is to have his first flight.

" Gee! " he told Clem after his first day, " it sure raises a sight of dust to git in a fellow's eyes, though."

Much as he loved tinkering with the brute, Rob soon lost his taste for working it. Like Thomas he complained it made him sick at his stomach. We got him goggles to wear over his eyes but he generally took them off. The dust and sweat covered them so he said he couldn't see how to drive.

Old Amos always referred to the tractor as " that there man killin' moneyeater."

We decided to sell or trade it if we could.

Before long Clyde and Rob sold it for us to a man over in the clay, " an old miserer," they said, " who would skin a flea for its hide and tallow." We had paid two hundred dollars for it two years ago and they sold

(269)

it for two hundred dollars. They got twenty-five dollars down. We offered them ten per cent for collecting the rest. They got eighty-five more.

By this time the new owner was tired of his bargain. He refused to pay another cent. Clem and I would have just let it go. We didn't like being beaten by the old miserer but it wasn't worth a lawsuit.

One morning we saw the tractor, sitting smugly in its accustomed place in our barn.

" He bring it back? " we asked, astounded.

" Not exactly, Cap," young Rob told us. " Clyde and me got pretty nigh drunk las' night and we knowed he wasn't goin' to pay no more money so we went over and brung it home."

Clem looked troubled. " Did you get a release, Rob? "

" Sure we did. Clyde held him and I done got twenty folks in off the highway to see him sign it. Here hit is."

Clem accepted it gracefully.

Young Rob said, " That old feller's so mean he'd drown little biddies in the creek."

Later I said, " Maybe he didn't have the money to pay up."

"He never intended to pay," Clem said. Clem is a Vermonter. He added, " Well, boys will be boys."

It became Rob's favorite toy. He liked to pump with

it and saw wood. Once in a great while he could even be persuaded to take it out and plough, if we were in a push and couldn't finish up with the horses.

To have out-traded that old miserer! It was the high spot of our farming career. I got a big kick out of it.

27

Sam was the son of the colored family who had share-cropped cotton with us and who still hung on in the cabin. Rob and he used to go hunting for squirrels and rabbits. Warren went along with them every now and then. It was great fun for him, and Clem and I felt he was plenty old enough to learn about the woods. I remembered hearing my father say that many of the happiest days he had had as a youngster were spent in the woods with a darky boy and an old hound dog.

Warren should have been in school. He was now six years old. But the nearest school was seven miles away and while the school bus would stop for him he would be at school or on the bus from half-past seven in the morning 'til nearly five in the afternoon. I was teaching him at home instead. On the farm, however, he was missing the greatest toy a small boy can have, a gang of other small boys.

One day he came home from an expedition with Rob and Sam, his eyes big with excitement. " And Clemmy," he said, " Rob jumped the log across the branch. And Sam said, ' I can do that. Watch me.' And then Clemmy, Sam took his gun and threw it clean over and it hit sup'm and went off, bang! Like that! " He stopped for breath.

" What did Rob do, Warren? "

" Rob hollered at him, ' you gol damn fool you, them shot went a-singin' past my ear. I've half a mind to beat you up proper.' He was scared but I wasn't."

Clem and I looked at each other. " They're just careless boys," he said to me. " But I'll speak to them both. Any fool ought to know better than to throw a loaded gun."

A day or so later when I saw the boys I began with, " Been throwing any more guns around, Sam? "

" No ma'm," said Sam.

Rob grinned. " Mr. Ripley done talked to us a-plenty, Miz Ripley, and I beat up Sam. Ain't that right, Sam? "

Sam looked a bit sheepish but he grinned and nodded.

Little Sally, our colored girl, was going to marry Sam. I used to hear him at night plinking on a little banjo at her house. There'd be a pause in the monotonous tune, the sound of a scuffle and a loud, " Aw you quit, Sam. Be-have yourself," from Sally, followed by peals of loud laughter from them both.

Sam was good to Warren. He used to carve pipes with old men's faces on them out of grindstone for him. They had stems of reed. Days he wasn't working he'd sit on the kitchen steps with old Sarah and Sally and watch Warren blow soap bubbles. The three darkies and Warren would laugh and shriek until they were weak over an untimely broken bubble. Mentally they seemed about the same age.

One evening Sally brought Sam in to see us. He stood behind her in the doorway, tall and shy with a pleasant sort of fatuous grin on his black face.

" Mist' Ripley," Sally said, " seems like Sam's found him an oil mine. Do you reckon you can fix it so's him, and you a'cos, kin make some cash money? "

Sam shuffled forward and brought Clem a shoe box of stones.

" Cain't you see oil a-shinin' through, Mist' Ripley? " he asked eagerly. " I know a place where all the ground's like that. It's a big oil mine."

We knew the stuff wasn't oil, of course, and undoubtedly was nothing of any value, but Clem promised to send the pebbles up to Raleigh and find out

(274)

about them. He was so eager we hated to disillusion him at once.

"Let him and Sally have some fun anticipating a fortune for a little while anyway," Clem said. "You can't tell, he or any of us may be dead before I hear it's no good. Let 'em have their fun while they can."

It was the middle of the next afternoon. I heard the shot plainly but country people were shooting quail and rabbits in the woods about us all through the winter and I thought nothing of it.

Ten minutes later I saw Berta, Sam's half crazy mother, run past the window. There was a sound of high, excited voices in the kitchen.

"Mrs. Ripley!" Old Sarah stood in the doorway. Her hands trembled. Her black face was a queer lusterless, sooty color. "Berta says, do come quick this minute, ma'm. Sam's shot hisself." She burst into sobs and threw her apron over her face.

"Shut up!" I said. "Find Mr. Ripley quick and Mr. Britt. Where's Sam?"

"Sally's gone lookin' for Mr. Ripley," Sarah sobbed. "Do Lord he'p the po' boy. His ma's gone back to 'im. He's laying out by the barn."

At that minute Clem came in. "Got some iodine, Katti? He's shot in the belly. In the army they told us to pour in iodine first thing."

(275)

"You go on down," I said. "I'll bring you the bottle."

I found them all at the barn. Clem, Old Man Britt, half-demented Berta, Sally and old Sarah.

Sam was lying at full length on the ground. Our automobile rug was under him. He had been sick all over it. His eyes stared wonderingly at us, like a trusting animal who is in pain and just hopes somebody will make it stop.

I looked away while Clem poured in the iodine. I heard the boy's choked gasp.

Old Amos shook his finger at him. "Well Sam," he said, "this had oughta teach you. Ef you'd ha' been over to the tar kiln a-workin' with yore pa where you'd oughta been, this 'ud never a-happened."

Sarah and Sally were weeping. Berta swayed to and fro mumbling and wringing her hands.

Old Amos said, "He was holdin' the pistol a-pointin' in his belly, cleanin' it, Cap."

I heard Clem say, "Sam, you fool, didn't you know enough to see whether the pistol was loaded before you started to clean it?"

Sam whispered, "Yes suh, I knowed it was loaded, Mist' Ripley."

Young Rob drove up with Dr. Kennedy. The doctor made a brief examination.

"I'll be fair with you, Mr. Ripley," he said. "I can't

handle it. They'll have to operate. You best take him to High Point."

Berta screamed. "Don't let 'em copperate him, Mist' Ripley. Don't let 'em copperate Sam."

Dr. Kennedy was staring down at the mess Sam had made on the rug. He turned to Clem. "Look at that stuff. Not a thing but hominy. Cotton crop ain't been so good. Niggers kinda in a tight this year."

Clem said, "What do I owe you, Doctor, for this visit?"

"'Bout three dollars, I reckon, Mr. Ripley. I reckon that boy's goin' to get well and be able to work it out for you."

"You hear that, Berta — Doctor says he's going to be all right. You hear that, Sam?"

Berta moaned and sobbed. Sam managed a "Yes, ma'm, I heered him. But I done heerd that bullet snap against my backbone. I reckon I'm a-goin' to die."

By this time Alex, Sam's father, had come. He was a sensible darky. He didn't say a word, but when Clem nodded to him he and the doctor helped Sam into the car. Sam leaned back against Alex's shoulder, groaning. Old Amos climbed in front by Clem.

It is more than sixty miles to High Point. They had a flat tire twenty miles before they got there. Sam groaned and prayed aloud all the way. Alex sat quietly

(277)

with his mouth set. Old Amos hunched forward and stared at the road ahead. Clem drove.

They got him to the hospital alive. The doctors did operate and they were sanguine about his chances. But he died next day.

Clem drove Alex back to make the funeral arrangements. Rob followed with the truck to bring back the body.

Sally showed no sign of grief and went about her work as usual.

Berta brought back my automobile rug, washed and ironed.

Alex borrowed the price of the coffin from Clem and asked for an old suit to bury Sam in. I gave him a green one, a second-hand gift from Clem's father, with a London tailor's name in it.

They had a big funeral and howled and sang far into the night. Some of the mourners stole Warren's two pet hens from their roost.

I told Clem, " I'm one of the few Southerners who confesses frankly that I do not in the least understand colored people."

Like everything else on the farm it became a story, a humorous story, to tell at Pinehurst dinner parties. Old Amos shaking his finger at the boy and pointing a moral as he lay in almost his last agony. Sam's meek, " I knowed it was loaded."

(278)

I caught myself a week later telling it at the Tufts', just as a colored waitress passed me something. Suddenly it flashed through my mind, "Probably this girl knew him. Maybe they were friends." I wondered, "Have I got thoroughly hardened — is this what living close to beautiful nature has done to me?"

The colored girl was faintly grinning. "We're all heartless," I thought. "Whether she knows him or not, he's one of her race."

I finished the story and everybody laughed and I felt heartily ashamed of myself. He was a darn decent, nice boy.

Warren often said, "Gee, I wish Sam was still here."

Alex and Berta moved out of the cabin one spring day. Alex never paid back the money he borrowed but we never really had any idea he would. Since Sam's death he did his work mechanically (he was working out the loan) but there was no heart in him.

28

Spring came again, '28, and our crop looked good.

What with one thing and another we knew we should spend close to three thousand on the year's orchard operations before the actual crop expenses. Thomas had been extravagant while we were away in the summer. Fertilizer was high that year. Sam's death had cost us fifty or sixty dollars. Our water tank had been blown down and had had to be replaced. There was a hundred dollars spent in repairs for the truck. And so on.

We looked forward to the peach season. Our friends, the growers who had gone away to work in the cities, came back to take off their crops. It was a reunion. For those two or three weeks the Sandhills had once again the pleasant, natural, country life atmosphere we had found when we first came down. There would be parties and informal dances and the free and easy flow of talk of people whose tastes and interests are the same, in a word, people who know and understand one another's viewpoint.

Having made money last season, we clung unreasonably to the hope that, in spite of the alarming rumors of a big crop all over the country, we'd make money again. That's the confirmed farmer for you. Facts and figures said clearly that we could not show a profit for '28 but as long as there's a farmer's God who hardly ever aims to hit a man, there is always a chance that he'll send hail or an earthquake or some bolt from the blue to wipe out the other fellow's crop.

The further the season advanced, the better our fruit looked. It wouldn't ripen for another month but by the end of June our green Elbertas were big enough to have packed a two-two pack.

Many of the Sandhill orchards were being attacked this season by a peach disease called bacteriosis. This disease does not hurt the fruit for eating, but it ruins its looks completely. Except in the early stages it is useless to ship such fruit, and even then, of course, it must sell at a discount. Peaches sell almost entirely on looks. The consumer buys the pretty ones.

Probably because we were well off the highway and far removed from other orchards, we were free from bacteriosis. Even in a year of bad prices, we thought, extra good fruit should bring a premium.

The American Growers' inspector came over to the packhouse the day before we expected to get our second full car. Big peaches that would pack a two-one (and Belles are generally a small peach) with flaming cheeks almost as red as Elbertas (and the chief trouble with Belles usually is that they haven't enough color) were rolling gently down the grading table.

" Aren't they beauties? " I said.

He nodded. " They've got the most color of any Belles I've seen this season." He hesitated. He picked up one or two from the picking boxes, glanced at them, and let them drop listlessly. He seemed to reach a sudden decision. " I'll be fair with you, Mrs. Ripley. I'd leave that car on the trees, if I were you. It won't pay you to pick and pack it."

" What do you mean? " I said. " Not pick and pack this fruit? It's the best we've ever had. You just said so yourself. You people get your commission anyway, no matter how little the cars bring. What do you mean, telling me not to ship? "

" That's just it, Mrs. Ripley. We would get a commission on anything that car brought above freight, but I just hate to see you people lose on it. I don't know what they'd say at the office, but I'm telling you you can't get enough out of these Belles in this market to pay for picking and packing them. Let your crew go now and get 'em back and crop your Elbertas, but don't

(282)

fool with these Belles. I've been handling truck all my life and I know. Your good stuff and the other fellow's bad stuff, when there's too much of it, is all dumped into the river together."

" Go look through the orchard," I said. " There's another whole car of Belles still hanging on those trees, as pretty fruit as there is in the Sandhills. If you think we'd just leave them hanging there why you're crazy, that's all. We've got to ship them."

He smiled wearily. " That's what they all say."

But we were stubborn. We told the gang to come back Monday as usual. This was Saturday.

" Maybe he's right," Clem said. " I don't know, probably is. But I'd rather lose money than leave fruit like this to rot on the trees."

I agreed. Of course, neither of us believed we would actually lose. " Think of what you'd pay for them in the North," I said.

It made us both laugh. That and the one about " Why don't you put up a canning factory? " will either bring a smile or the fighting look to the face of any Sandhills grower. All the men who came down always suggested a canning factory as a brilliant and original idea that would solve all our problems.

Of course, it had been tried. There were two reasons why it was bound to fail. First, there was nothing for the factory to do except during the short season. Second,

(283)

our peaches are not canning peaches. They can only be put up as a mixture for cheap jam or to fill pies. The canning peach, neatly sliced in halves, is a special variety grown for that purpose.

The women always told us how expensive peaches were in the Northern markets. " Just think, you sell a bushel for a dollar," they'd say. " And in New York we pay a dollar for a little basket like this." (Business with hands.)

Having decided to ship the Belles anyway we tried to forget the " damnpeaches " over Sunday (like " damnyankees," it had become one word) and drove over to the Derbys' for dinner.

Of course, I couldn't forget the peaches and I talked about them. " If it wasn't that they're so pretty this year I wouldn't really care so much," I said.

Roger looked thoughtful. " I'm going to make you a suggestion," he said. " You may want to take it and you may not. I sold, two months ago, eighteen carloads of peaches, Belles at a dollar and a quarter a crate, Elbertas at a dollar seventy-five, to Martin and Martin, the New York commission men. I'll tell you what I'll do. My fruit has been hard hit by bacteriosis. If your fruit's as good as you say it is, I'll let you in on this contract. Naturally, now the price has dropped so low, they'll kick over the contract if they can. You take that chance. You'll have to ship in crates instead of bushels,"

(284)

Roger went on, "and ship under the Carolina Club label. The cars load at Jackson Springs. I can lend you some professional packers."

We looked over the contract.

"All right," Clem said, "Thanks a lot, Roger. We'll ship with you."

I said, "Roger, like Mr. Micawber, I'm beginning to believe something will always turn up."

We worked out the details. By tomorrow morning our packhouse, equipped solely for busheling, our labor, trained only to bushel, would have to turn to crates.

It was suggested that we haul the picking boxes over to George Maurice's (the Maurices were shipping with Roger) and pack there where they were equipped for crates. Clem was enthusiastic about the idea. I didn't think it would work. I had handled the practical end of packing and I knew the local labor. I wasn't very clear in my own mind just what my objections were. I was persuaded. At least I was completely out-argued.

It was early the next morning, hardly daylight, when I heard a car rumble past my window. A few minutes later old Amos was calling outside. "Cap! Cap! I want to talk to you."

I could hear the murmur of their voices — Amos' worried and excited, Clem's soothing, but with more of a hint of annoyance in it.

"Well, I look to you, Cap," I heard Amos say.

(285)

" He is a bad'un, I know, but you and me'll have to see him through."

Clem came in and began putting on his clothes.

" What's the trouble, Clem? " I asked.

" What would it be? Young Rob. The damn fool was out in that tin can of his last night with another boy, and now the boy is dead."

" Oh Clem! And young Rob? "

" He's in jail. Where would he be? "

" Is he hurt? "

" Of course not. You couldn't kill him. The car's a wreck. They had no lights and were both drunk. I'm sorry for old Amos. He's done his best for his boys. But I wish to God I knew where I was going to get another truck driver."

" Can't you bail him out? "

" I haven't got time. Can you spare Clyde? "

" I guess I'll have to."

" He'll have to drive the truck. God help the truck. Amos is pretty well cut up, poor old fellow."

It was the first incident in a day of calamities. We were in what is described locally as " a strut " by day-light — Amos, the wagon driver, sick with worry and fear for his boy, Clyde suddenly put in charge of the truck, an old bundle of iron, whose idiosyncrasies only young Rob understood thoroughly.

At seven o'clock, with the best smile I could muster,

the kind school teachers use when they tell the children they'll all have to come back Saturday to rehearse the dear little class song they're going to sing for Commencement, I broke the news to the packhouse gang that we'd pack today at Mr. Maurice's. I tried to make it sound like a treat.

The girls were silent. They looked very doubtful. Then they began to talk all at once. They insisted they'd told pa and ma they were a-goin' to work at Mr. Ripley's and they couldn't tell if pa and ma'd like it if they went over somewheres else. Several of them had brought their lunches in the same boxes with their fathers' and brothers' who were pickers. They said they couldn't divide the lunch. I promised that Sarah would feed the men at the house if they'd go. Cora Lee Dunn, one of the two ringers, who was a trained packer and on whom I was counting to pack, said flatly she wouldn't go. She made first one excuse and then another. She'd " taken with the headache." She hadn't worn a clean dress, and she was ashamed to be seen on the highway in the one she was wearing. Finally I persuaded her to whisper to me the real reason.

" Their packhouse, I've heered, is up on stilts, Miz Ripley. It's such a hot day," she giggled — " I didn't wear no pants."

I lent her pants.

One man just plain quit, but Clyde and I herded the

(287)

rest, about twenty people, together, and he drove them over in the truck.

We packed in a small auxiliary packhouse of the Maurices'. It was fine except for two things. The first appeared trifling but it proved to be upsetting: The Maurices did not give their hands iced water in the packhouse. Most of the packhouses do. Our gang was used to it. All day long they grumbled. Cora Lee said she felt faint without it. I had to keep my temper. To jolly them along. If they left, where would we go in the height of the season for labor?

Our people weren't getting on with the Georgia professional packers Roger had sent over, either. The Georgia packers too, had not wanted to come, and were sullen at having to work for a woman. They were used to working in gangs in a big packhouse under their own Georgia boss who hired and fired them, and to whom they were directly responsible. They shirked and grumbled as much as they dared. We were of course very short-handed.

But the serious difficulty was the lack of a telephone. There was none nearer than the Maurices' house about half a mile away. I had no way of keeping in touch with the orchard or of gauging how much fruit to expect.

Clem was at the loading station at Jackson Springs. Dunc Britt, the picking boss, was lost, as the seven-mile haul each way soon used up the picking boxes.

(288)

This meant that the pickers were, after the first few loads went, short of boxes as the empties could not be brought back fast enough. Dunc sent word that the gang had to stop picking, as there were no boxes to put the peaches in.

" Clyde, tell him to use his head. Get bushel baskets and pick in those," I sent word back but there had already been the delay.

" And Dunc says to tell you," Clyde said, when he came back with the next load, " them baskets don't load right."

Sure enough they didn't. Picking boxes can be stacked one above the other in the truck. The bushels were not strong enough to stack.

I spent the noon hour driving about from orchard to orchard trying to find somebody who was overstocked with picking boxes, and who would sell or rent me some. Mr. Jesse Page, who had helped us out of difficulties before, was kind enough to lend me fifty for the rest of the day. Even so this meant another delay while the truck made a trip to get them.

The truck, however, rose nobly to the occasion and as Clyde put it, " The old thing sure is puttin' out."

We were in a push that afternoon right. The orchard swamped us with fruit. We had to rent two extra trucks to help with the hauling.

In the midst of the Belles a load of Elbertas came.

(289)

They were enormous peaches from a few trees that for some reason bore early.

Roger happened over to see how we were getting on. " Those big beauties are too big to pack," he said.

" Sure," I said. " We're going to bushel them."

" That seems a pity with such beautiful fruit. I tell you what, why don't you ring them up in bushel baskets by hand? They'll be something extra fancy to sweeten the cars. They can ride on top of the crates in an Elberta car we're loading."

I demurred tactfully, thinking how clean and fresh Roger looked in his linen suit, and how crumpled I must appear in my peach-stained smock with the sweat pouring down my face. I felt myself at a disadvantage. I made the first excuse that came into my mind. " There's no one here knows how to ring up from the bottom."

" Nonsense," Roger said. " The Georgia boys do. Come on over, boys. Let's ring up these Elbertas. We used to do it years ago at Derby Farm."

The girl packers who were left alone at the packing table looked at me. The bins were full now to overflowing. The full picking boxes of Belles were stacked high. The local boys, the crate topper, the boy who lifted the boxes, the others who as a personal favor to me and because Clyde threatened them with hard fists, were helping out and grading with the girls, looked toward

(290)

me. Clyde, who had just come up with a load began,
" But Miz Ripley, the Belles is plenty to keep us . . ."
A Georgia packer nudged his neighbor.

I knew Roger was one of the best peach men in the
section but he was used to doing things on a large scale,
with plenty of labor. Our little packhouse was a
very different proposition from his, especially pushed
as we were today. But I wanted to do what he suggested. After all we were darn lucky to be in on his
contract.

In the whole afternoon the three Georgia professionals
ringed from the bottom just fifteen bushels. They purposely slacked on the work as they resented having to
leave the big Derby packhouse, but ringing bushels up
from the bottom is a particularly slow pack.

In desperation we threw the rest into the grading
table at last and just ringed the tops as we were accustomed to.

We stopped in the black dark. The truck headlight
threw huge shadows over the little packshed. The place
was ankle deep in peaches. Everything was topsy-turvy.
The men and girls stumbled from fatigue as they
climbed on the truck.

" Miz Ripley, I can't come tomorra if we're goin' to
pack here," from several.

" Miz Ripley, we git overtime, don't we? " from
others.

(291)

"Miz Ripley, Pa ain't going to like it me comin' home so late. What'll I tell him?"

Dunc sent word that a cull buyer was coming to buy a truck load of soft peaches. I waited an hour in the cool dark.

Have I hated today so just on account of the hard work and petty annoyances or is it all really as futile as it seems to me? Stop thinking, I told myself. A tune they used to play at dances just after the war had been humming through my brain all day. In a minute I'd remember the words.

> "There's a lot of peaches down in Georgia.
> Have a peach of a time —
> Dum, dum, dum —
> I know a little peach just seventeen,
> I think that peach is a little too green —
> There's a lot of peaches down in Georgia."

I was wearing a white dress with black lace. The men were all in uniform. There was the intoxication of the sway of dancing bodies. The insistent beat of the music. "Everything is peaches down in Georgia." I was back where it was just one of a dozen tunes to dance by.

I sat bolt upright suddenly on the sawdust floor of the packhouse. Clem and I met at that dance. . . . Well here we were. Funny where following an apparently idle train of thought will bring you up.

(292)

I said to myself, " It'll be easier at home tomorrow. You're just tired now but if the peaches don't pay expenses we'll have to go back to the old treadmill of living on borrowed money. You've got to do what you can to make 'em pay." I can telegraph to Fort Valley, I thought, and get a good reliable packhouse boss to come up. No more fuzzy peaches for me. Clean clothes and a book and pillows behind my head in the swing. Say it would cost roughly two hundred dollars for the season. The extra equipment and labor he'd require that I'd manage to do without would perhaps cost another hundred. We were running behind. Today had probably, first and last, amounted to a hundred dollars more than it should have. No, this was my job. I could do it and I would. But after this I'd do it my own way.

I heard the rattle of the cull buyer's car.

" Hello," he called out.

" You remember me, Miz Ripley," he said. " I bought peaches from you last year and you give me a kitten."

" Oh sure I do. You're Mr. McKenna. How's the kitten? "

" Hog ate that one. I was plum sorry. I sure like them funny feets them cat's got. Your nigger cook gimme another one though. She's in a sack."

I heard a faint mew from the car.

I wanted to say, give it back — you won't take good

care of it. But I couldn't hurt the well meaning fellow's feelings. Maybe it wasn't his fault the hog got the other. Oh well, what's a kitten — we had to dispose, one way or another, of four batches a year.

He only wanted six bushels of culls, and on the strength of having taken the kitten, and bought peaches last year, and the lateness of the hour, he, in local parlance, " done beat me down " to twenty cents a bushel.

I had waited two hours, without supper and since I'd been trying to get hold of picking boxes at lunch time I had missed my lunch too, for a dollar and twenty cents.

Clem stopped for me on his way back from the loading station.

" Clem," I said. " Never again. We pack at home tomorrow."

We left behind us bushels and bushels of culls. Our regular cull buyers had come to our own packhouse and had the culls been there we might have sold them. As it was the trucks had more than they could do hauling the peaches from the field and to the loading station, so we lost the culls, part of the waste of that day.

It was a lot easier afterwards, back at our own place. Roger sent us other packers who were easier to deal with.

The fruit was beautiful. More beautiful that year than any. The peaches were big and brilliantly colored. To walk through the Elberta orchard was to walk through a Maxfield Parrish painting. The American Growers sent buyers to see the luscious fruit hanging on the trees. Other growers got us to send flats of them as presents to their friends.

A dollar and seventy-five cents was no sort of price.

" It does seem a pity we couldn't have had this fancy stuff last year when the price was up," I said to Clem.

" Better thank your stars you've got it this year," Clem said. " It's the only thing that got us on this contract — and without the contract we'd be sunk. Bushel baskets of fruit like this were bringing eighty cents f.o.b. yesterday. And that inspector who told you to leave the Belles on the trees was right, too. The market reports show we'd have got a return of forty-five cents a bushel for them in the open market."

" That's so," I said. I knew we couldn't even pick and pack a bushel for less than fifty cents.

Clem was frowning. " The thing I'm afraid of is that we may not be able to collect the contract," he said. " You know Martin and Martin are trying to jump it, I s'pose? "

I didn't think they could. It said plainly, " Fruit must pass Government inspection U. S. No. 1 f.o.b. Jackson Springs." All our fruit had passed I knew. " Hasn't Roger's fruit passed? " I asked.

" Oh yes," Clem said. " The Carolina Club is only putting their best stuff in those cars. It's all good."

(295)

" Well? " I said.

" I'll wait 'til I have my check," Clem said, " before I celebrate."

Roger telephoned us a day or so later to come over to his place. Clem was right. Martin and Martin were crawfishing. They were threatening to refuse the cars. The four or five growers who composed the Carolina Club looked glum.

" But Roger," I said, " we have an open and shut contract."

Roger explained patiently. " Yes, but they say the fruit hasn't been up to specifications when it reached them. It's a trumped up excuse — but what can we do? Suppose they simply refuse to accept the cars. They'll have to be auctioned off on the platform. They'll be massacred. We can sue Martin and Martin afterward, but — well, it will be a hard thing to prove, and suing is pretty expensive. The American Growers are handling this for us, of course."

" What do they advise? " Mr. Maurice asked.

" They advise us to compromise," Roger said.

" But it's absolutely unfair," I gasped. " Why should we compromise? We've fulfilled our share of the contract. Suppose the market had gone up instead of down wouldn't they have held us? "

Roger smiled. " Of course. But that isn't the point." He explained all over again. The commission men could and would, if pushed, throw over the contract. The cars sold in a hurry off the platform would bring practically nothing. We could sue for breach of contract. They'd fight it. Even if we won it would be an expensive lawsuit. It would be cheaper for us in the long run to lie down and take a cut.

" It's been done to the peach growers and truck growers over and over again," someone said.

" Then what's the good of a prior sale? " I asked. " It seems to me it's heads they win, and tails we lose."

" Perhaps, but it was a chance to get something better than the market," Clem said. " Maybe we won't get as much as we thought at first, but even with a big cut we'll be getting more for our fruit than if we didn't have the contract. See, Katti? "

Roger went to New York to fight it out with Martin and Martin. He wangled things so well that our Belles were cut only from a dollar and a quarter to eighty-five cents, and our Elbertas from a dollar seventy-five to a dollar fifty.

But the gyp rankled in my mind. I said to Clem, " It's because we're all farmers and have let ourselves slip into the farmer's way of looking at things. I don't believe for a minute a manufacturer would let a gyp like that be put over on him. But everybody imposes on the farmer and the farmer has just got used to it, and submits to it."

(297)

29

We dropped three thousand dollars in the year's farming operations ('28), excluding our living. Our returns came to something over three thousand dollars and we had spent better than six thousand. We did have most of our bushel baskets left over, but as it turned out we were unable to sell them and we have never used them.

At the end of the crop, Clem heard from a magazine to which he had submitted his first novel, " Dust and Sun," for serialization. They accepted it and paid him three thousand dollars. This cancelled off the orchard loss. We were just where we were years ago. We had no debts. We had no money in the bank. We were starting all over again.

And yet we weren't. There was a difference. After the sale of the novel, we were sure. It was no longer just a rosy hope, we both knew Clem could make a living out of writing.

" And I can sink all I make in the orchard," he said, " and we can go on giving up our lives as a sacrifice to peaches. No, I'm through. This year's taught me. I'd sell this place at any price. Will trade farm," he added, " for shot gun, dose of prussic acid, or what have you."

Seriously though it seemed the thing to do — to sell the farm for anything it would bring. We even considered abandoning the orchard and just living in the house.

" But Clem, we can't do that really though," I said. " Look at all we've sunk in it. Nobody knows what's going to happen. There are probably heaps of orchardists who can't hold on and who'll have to let their orchards go. We'll be among the few who held on, and make a killing if we stick."

It seemed almost inconceivable that an orchard such as ours, into which had gone more than thirty-three thousand dollars, including the farm and house, should not be worth keeping up on the chance of a good peach season.

The place was already listed for sale with every real estate agent for miles around. All the legitimate agents about us had had it listed for years. Clem even went now, as a sort of forlorn hope, to a little Jew, who traded parcels of land, houses, or anything else he could get his hands on.

The Jew said. " Vell, Mr. Ripley, I can try."

We had no real hope that he could sell it, but Clem told him, " If you can get any reasonable cash offer, I'll sell."

" Of course we've got to hang on," Clem said to me. " If we abandon the orchard all we'd have to offer for sale would be a poor man's sand farm, and you know what that'll bring. Just nothing. As long as we have the orchard, some poor sucker with a yen to grow peaches may come along. We can show him how much profit we made in '27."

Clyde came up to see me. " Miz Ripley, I'm saying good-bye. T'aint nothin' here for me. I'm goin' to try another hitch in the Marines."

Even Rob decided to leave. He'd only been out of jail a week or so. Clem had paid his lawyer's fees and costs, sixty dollars. Amos had guaranteed that Rob would work it out. Of course we knew, and so did old Amos, that he wouldn't.

" Mr. Ripley," the old man said, " if he don't work it out, you know I will."

We knew that too. " But I'd hate to collect from the old man," Clem said. " I knew that sixty was gone when I paid it."

I could see old Amos hated to have to come up and tell us that Rob had skipped.

" Cap, you give me time," he said. " I aim to pay

(300)

you back every cent of that sixty dollars Rob owes you."

" All right Amos," Clem said. " We'll fix that some way. Don't worry about it now. Where's he gone? "

" I don't rightly know. I reckon down to Georgia or somewheres."

" What's he going to do there? "

" Well Cap, I don't rightly know 'bout that. Git him a job long enough to buy him somethin' to eat and some gas, I reckon. Gertrude said he took his Bible along. He done told her if he should run out of money he could always go to preachin'."

We got the orchard cleaned up. Slack time began. Clem and I talked over what was to be done during the coming year. We decided to do just what was absolutely necessary to keep the trees in good shape, and let the rest of the farm pretty much go.

Clem had a talk with old Amos. " I can't afford to keep a man here by the month at regular wages," he told him. " You see how things are with peaches. If you want to stay on in the house and be paid for work by the day, when I need you, I'd like to have you stay."

Amos agreed to stay. Growers were cutting wages and turning off labor. It was hard to get a job.

" I hate to do it," Clem said. " But this farm now just won't support a fifty dollar a month man."

30

The end of September. Hot. Trees losing their leaves. Yellow weeds growing in the orchard. Water pump broken as usual and no water to bathe in.

The Sandhills was broke. My friends talked of opening shops, of starting kindergartens, of making various articles for sale. Each two or three gathered in a group, shook their heads over the circumstances of some other who wasn't present.

"Yes, they've lost everything. Did you know he had to stop shipping after the first week? Couldn't meet his payroll."

Talk of shaky banks. Of a whole group that broke one after the other, like beads dropping from a snapped string, in the peach section of Georgia, when the returns began to trickle in.

The same unasked question in everyone's mind: "Will the good years for peaches ever really come? Is it worth while to hold on? . . . How can we do anything but hold on? "

Our own petty difficulties. The trouble with the men who brought over the threshing machine to thresh our scanty oat crop. Amos' grumblings. Rob's crestfallen return to the farm after two weeks' absence. Preachin' couldn't have worked out so well.

The sun beat on the low roof of the house. Clem was in his office, half stripped, typing. I was hoeing about the roots of some drooping chrysanthemums, in an effort to encourage them to struggle on in spite of the heat. I heard the rattle of a car.

" Somebody's coming, Clem," I called.

Raising a great cloud of dust, up drove a shiny new Ford. Out hopped the little Jew who had said, " Vell, I'll try to sell your farm, Mr. Ripley." He was beaming. He was rubbing his hands together. He radiated good will and satisfaction.

" Vell, Mr. Ripley," he said, " I have sold your farm for you."

Clem grabbed hold of the door casing. " You have what? " he gasped.

" I have sold your place, Mr. Ripley," he repeated. " I have sold your place for ten thousand dollars."

Clem didn't hesitate. He fairly clutched the Jew's hand. " No wonder God chose you," he said. " You're a real genius."

(303)

Mr. Einstein came into the house with us.

"Now you understand, Mr. Ripley," he said, "I ain't got the money. What you must understand is, this here is a business deal. I'm goin' to tell you now how it all is."

At great length and with many gestures he told us. The buyers were a shaky real estate firm in Greensboro. They had a man they expected to work if off on at a profit. Einstein explained. "When he pays them, Mr. Ripley, they pay us. It sounds like funny business, but you know peach orchards ain't no easy thing to sell. You be thinking of that ten thousand dollars, cash money."

We were.

We went up to Greensboro with Einstein next day and signed a contract of sale. We were perfectly aware of the shaky character of the men we were dealing with. Einstein let slip doubts of their solvency. But we hadn't dared hope for a sale at all, much less ten thousand dollars for the place. We looked up the third man, for whom the signers of the contract were acting, and found he had a good rating. He was a wholesale hardware dealer or something.

The contract of sale was air tight. The third man, Mr. McCann, we'll call him, now came out in the open as the buyer. He told Clem he had bought out the interest of the other two. He even talked to Amos and arranged for him to stay on and run the place for him.

I happened to be in bed with a little cold the morning Mrs. McCann drove down with her husband to look over their new farm. I had told Sarah to show them over the house.

I could hear Mrs. McCann's little " ohs " and " ahs " of approval and fragments of sentences. There was something that sounded like this: " If we and the children really come down for week-ends — you'll have to change this — or that." And once, though I can't be sure, " Isn't it strange they didn't put all the books one height on the same shelf? So unneat. Poor things — probably didn't know any better."

" I can't see why they have so many books anyway," Mr. McCann boomed. " Should think they'd put them up in the lumber room, 'stead of having them cluttering up the whole side of a wall this way."

They were standing just outside my door now. I could hear their voices distinctly.

Sarah was saying, " Miz Ripley's in there. She ain't feeling so good today."

Mr. McCann said handsomely, " That's all right. Come on, honey."

Mrs. McCann's fluttery voice insisted, " She isn't really sick, is she? I don't believe she'd mind my just peeping in."

(305)

There was a light tap on the door.

Mr. McCann said, " Now, honey — "

I called, " Come in! "

She came, alone.

" Oh, Mrs. Ripley, I'm Mrs. McCann. I'm so sorry you aren't well." She broke off suddenly.

My room was severely simple, a plain walnut chest of drawers, a hooked rug, and me in bed with the covers up to my chin and my hair hanging in two long plaits. Her eyes left me to stare at something intently. My eyes followed hers. Mimi was curled on the foot of my bed. At first I thought she'd caught sight of Mimi's oversized feet. Most people stared when they did. But Mrs. McCann wasn't looking at Mimi. Her eyes were traveling first up and then down. Mrs. McCann was staring at the four posts of my bed.

It was a fairly good mahogany four-poster — nothing extraordinary. My great-grandmother, in her old age, had had the legs sawed off so she wouldn't have to climb so high, which destroyed its value. But Mrs. McCann had her eye on those posts. She had made a find.

Her voice fluttered more than ever as she said, " Would you care to sell any of your furniture with the house? "

That tone! The familiar careful casualness of it. The tone I'd used so often, the tone I knew so well in the

(306)

days I went antiquing. Somebody was playing my part. On an impulse that I couldn't resist I said, " Well ma'm, I don't rightly know. I ain't been figuring on it. But I might could let you have the cookstove, ma'm."

I had put her at her ease. A faintly amused, altogether satisfied, expression spread over her face. The look of the cat who has the mouse between its paws. She understood me.

" Well, I didn't mean your stove exactly, Mrs. Ripley," she simpered. " But now that bed you have, surely you don't want to have to move a big thing like that. I might be able to use it — to take it off your hands."

" Yes ma'm," I said.

" It's pretty old, of course," she hesitated. " Here's a scratched place, too." She shook her head sadly.

" Yes, ma'm," I said.

" I tell you what I'll do," she said. " I'll buy the bed from you and you won't have to be bothered with moving it, and can get a nice enameled one when you go to town. They are much more stylish now, you know. You'd like that wouldn't you? "

I knew I'd giggle. She was so exactly like me trying to buy the old country woman's walnut chest.

" What are you laughing for? " she asked.

I kicked at Mimi. " Cat tickled my toes," I said.

She smiled. She was all benevolence. " Why, I'll

give you — I'll give you twenty-five dollars for this bed," she said. " It's a lot, but I want you to be able to get an up-to-date, modern one for yourself."

" What you want with this old wreck? " I asked. " The posts is warped plum anti-Godly-wise."

" It is an old wreck of course," she said. " It does seem strange to like old things better than new, doesn't it? I can't explain why I like them. But you just think of all you can do with twenty-five whole dollars."

I nodded. " Yes, ma'm." I hesitated. Words from long ago came to me. " But if you want hit, I want hit," I said. And because I couldn't help it I began to laugh.

She looked at me a little oddly. She was puzzled and ill at ease. She opened her mouth as if to say something and shut it again. Just a small town woman, old enough to be my mother, unimaginative but probably well meaning in her own way. She was a little pathetic. I wished I could crawl altogether under the covers.

She was fumbling for words. " Well, good-bye, Mrs. Ripley. I am most pleased to have met you," she said.

It's queer how we all cling to our formulas when we feel at sea.

She turned back as she reached the door. As though the words had been jerked out of her in spite of herself, she said, " I suppose you just wanted to live out here way away in the country. I guess — why I reckon — maybe there are people who just do like it."

(308)

31

A few days later, Clem and I began to pack up our things. We hadn't got the money yet, but we knew McCann had plenty and he had told us he was the real purchaser.

The regrets we had in leaving the farm were swallowed up in the thrill of having got rid of it without having to call it a dead loss. We were still dazed by the miracle of the sale.

It was pouring rain as we packed to go. From the various places there was the drip, drip, drip, we had grown accustomed to. Clem looked at them with a beatific expression. " It's McCann's roof now."

" The rain's going to help the holly trees we transplanted," I ventured.

We looked at each other.

" Katti, you and I would be well rid of this farm if we never got a cent for it. We'd be richer than we are today if at any time in the last few years we'd had the nerve simply to walk out and turn the key behind us. I'm a writer and we're going where I can have time to think and write. We have finished with farming."

I knew it was all true. Warren could go to school with a gang of other youngsters. Clem could be near a reference library. The butcher and grocer would deliver at our door. The postman would stop with the mail.

We rented a little house and moved to Charleston. We smelled the damp salt air again and felt the pavements under our feet. We liked to turn on the water full force and let it run loud and long. Just snapping the electric light buttons was a thrill.

A month slid by. The day came around for the money to be paid. Instead of a check only a worried letter came from Einstein.

" I'll have to run up and see about it," Clem decided.

When he came back he was worried too. " Had to give them more time," he told me. " The two real estate agents haven't anything. The only solvent one of the trio is McCann. I hope this farm hasn't got a rubber on it."

Thirty days later the second date for payment came and again there was a flimsy excuse and no check. Clem went up to see McCann. He came back sadly crestfallen. He told me this time that McCann wept. He complained that the Jew and the real estate men had misrepresented things.

" Why, Mr. Ripley, I've been asking 'round and they tell me there's no money in peaches. What if I am getting a forty thousand dollar place for ten thousand dollars; it's no good to me if I can't make it pay. My bank refused to lend more than twenty-five hundred dollars on it."

When Clem repeated it to me I said, " Weren't you touched? What did he expect? "

" Oh he's just one of those big busy business men who's made a small fortune out of hardware, or whatever it is, and had an idea he could buy a farm cheap, put in a man to run it, and take out twenty percent a year, while he used the house as sort of a play place for week-ends. It never seemed to occur to him that if that could be done, I'd be doing it." He laughed. " Poor soul! Another complaint he had was that Mrs. McCann hadn't liked it. You'd better have thrown in the bed, Katti."

Clem found we'd have to sue to enforce the contract. He put the affair with all its ramifications in the hands of a lawyer. It's still there. The farm did have a rubber attached to it. It snapped right back to us.

We decided, now we were in Charleston and had leased a house we might as well spend the winter. Clem could drive up every week or so (it only takes

(311)

five hours) and see what Amos was doing. We'd go back for the peach season as so many of our friends had been doing for years.

Charleston is a pleasant, mellow old city. We spent a placid winter, but we missed Pinehurst, and we missed the excitement of farming. Life was easier but we missed the freedom of the country. The sunshine glinting on the white sand that was all our own. The clean wind that blew across our own land. The hundred-acre block of air that we owned, including the chunk of blue sky above. The quail and rabbits and funny little field mice which were ours. The fields that might lie fallow or be put to work to grow crops just as we decided.

" Wait a minute right there," Clem said. " It sounds fine. But just take those crops you're talking about. Did they ever pay enough to be worth while? There's one thing to remember about farming, Katti. Never get romantic or sentimental about it. Sure as you do it will backfire at you."

Clem and I spent many hours in fruitless arguments on farming in general and our own farm in particular.

For five years, we had been hearing that in three years time enough peach orchards would be forced out of business by the poor prices to curb the overproduction and bring back an era of normal times to the peach indus-

(312)

try. The experts had been telling the growers that since '24.

Now they were still saying prosperity was three years ahead of us, and yet we knew of dozens of men who had gone broke growing peaches, and who had either sold their orchards or let the banks, their creditors, take them over for the mortgages. It must have been even more true of Georgia, than of the Sandhills.

The salient point was, we decided, that although the individual did go broke, the orchard continued to produce. The original owner or the bank sold it for say half what it would cost to plant and bring it into bearing. There is always a fellow who thinks that if he can buy a business at fifty cents on the dollar he can make money. The men who bought peach orchards on that basis discovered shortly that they couldn't, but they in turn found someone who thought he could grow peaches at a profit if he got his orchard at twenty-five cents on the dollar. Somebody kept the orchards going. Even " abandoned " orchards, in which nothing was done to prevent the spread of disease and worms, would often for a year or so bear quantities of wormy, inferior fruit, which somebody thought worth picking and shipping.

If a factory fails and a bank takes it over, most likely the raw material is sold to one person, the machinery to another, and the building is used for an entirely different purpose. But this is not true of a farm. Once a farm always a farm.

If worst comes to the worst, a tenant can always be found to buzzard a peach orchard, that is, live on it a year or so and pay the taxes for what he can make out of the fruit. It sometimes takes several years for a neglected orchard to go out of bearing completely. Meantime the fruit is so ridden with diseases and pests it is practically uneatable and the trees are a menace to near-by orchards. Up to now comparatively few orchards had been cut down compared with the number that were being given a lick and a promise on the chance of some optimist running into a string of lucky circumstances and making a profit.

We heard the truck farmers about Charleston complain of their crops, potatoes, tomatoes, egg plants, cabbages, in the same terms we used of peaches. Unless some other section suffered calamity, the growers lost money. In a normal year overproduction often makes it useless to harvest a crop. The cabbage or whatever it is rots in the fields.

Our system of farm relief, that consists in giving banks more money to lend to farmers to plant more crops when there is already overproduction, does not seem to get anywhere near the root of the trouble.

Being no economist, I cannot argue the theory of farm relief, but I've watched the results. I've seen a pretty respectable Sandhill cotton farmer relieved to the point where he doubled his little crop, hit a year when everyone else did the same, and next season had his fifteen-year-old daughter behind the plough not a hundred feet from the Raleigh-Charlotte highway. Loans to help a grower hang on will not help in the long run. The sooner enough orchards go out to bring the production of peaches down to a point where they will sell and give the grower a fair return, the better for all orchardists. The hope of good prices that depends on an accident of weather or disease to some other grower's crop is not only a mirage but unsound business.

But in the spring the prospect for peaches looked good. I had a sneaking feeling of gladness that McCann hadn't come through, and we had the farm still. Once a farmer always a farmer. It's something I cannot explain. What draws a man who has lost time after time back again to the stock market?

32

We moved home again to Samarcand in the late spring of '29 to get ready to ship our crop.

" How are you, Amos? And how's Rob? And how's Gertrude? "

Gertrude was Amos' sixteen-year-old daughter and the apple of his old eye.

He grinned. " Rob and me are all right, Miz Ripley. And Gert — why Gert's just fine. She's fatter than a hog."

It was good to be home again.

The Southern peach crop in '29 was infested with worms. After the disastrous season of '28, most growers had economized on their orchards. Many had let the drops stay on the ground after the crop. Others had not sprayed or dusted in the spring. The worms had bred in the many neglected and dying orchards and had infected nearly all the fruit everywhere.

" Whoever has clean fruit this season is going to make money," said the government experts and marketing agencies.

Again our isolated situation had protected us. Old Amos said, " Yes sir, Cap, there's been worms, but I been after them so hard they's plum scared to show their ugly faces. When Rob dusts them trees with poison dust, the worms come just a-boilin' out." The old man had done a good job with the trees and done it cheaply.

Clem came in from Candor one day wearing a broad grin. " Katti, did you hear about the man who gave a fellow ten bushels of peaches to make into brandy for him? "

" No, I'll bite."

" Brought him back one pint of liquor."

" Well? I don't see — "

" Neither did the peach grower. He said, ' Is this all I get? ' ' No, sir,' the moonshiner told him, ' besides that pint of liquor I made from the peaches, you get nine and a half buckets of lard I made out of the worms.' Laugh, Katti, it's funny."

" Has everybody got wormy fruit, Clem? "

" The section's riddled with 'em. Cheer up, we've got clean fruit compared with most."

In spite of the worms there was the same thrill of excitement in the air as in '27. The market was up due to the very short crop. Everywhere the trees were set

(317)

light after the bumper crop they had borne in '28. There was feeling among a good many peach men that since there were so few peaches, if the public couldn't get clean fruit, it would perforce buy wormy fruit. One frank soul put it aptly, " Sure what's a worm? He's born in the peach, lives in the peach, he's just all peach, ain't he? "

" If there's any truth in the fable of the man who made a better mousetrap and the world flocking to his door, with our sound clean fruit we surely ought to make a killing this season," I said to Clem.

" I figure between two and three thousand net," Clem said. " Georgia Elbertas are bringing two fifty a crate now."

Clem had come out pretty well with his writing lately and I had become a lady again after six months away from the farm. We engaged a Georgia foreman to handle the packhouse. Dunc Britt came up from the sawmill in South Carolina where he had been working to handle the picking gang. Dunc was a hard worker. He was a square-jawed, ex-infantry sergeant. This he told Clem, was his summer vacation. With a good pack-house boss and a good picking foreman, it looked as though this would be a season when Clem and I could sit back and take it easy, and just count the money clinking into the bank.

The high spot of the season that stands out in my

mind was the battle between old Amos and Dunc that started things off with a bang.

Clem was at the loading station. It was about eleven o'clock in the morning. I was writing letters and my mind was far from peaches, when old Amos, without even knocking, opened the door and stalked in.

" Miz Ripley, where's Cap? I want to see him private." I saw his hands were trembling.

" Why you know, Amos, over at the Belle Berta siding, isn't he? "

" Well it don't make no difference no ways," Amos said. " You kin tell Cap, I'm quittin'. I'll take Rob with me I reckon, but I'll make him send Cap the rest of that money he owes him. You tell Cap we're goin'."

" Amos," I said, " have you lost your mind? "

" No, ma'm, but I can't work with Dunc. You tell Cap that."

" Now Amos," I began, " what'll we do? Who'll drive the wagon? Who'll drive the truck? What — "

I heard the car come up and creak to a stop. Clem came in. I got up to leave.

" I've been talking to Dunc, Amos — " Clem said.

" Yes sir," old Amos interrupted. " I reckon he's been a-tattlin'. That so and so — "

Clem grinned. " After all he's your own son."

" Well Cap, I can't work with that boy — "

I tiptoed away.

(319)

Clem told me the rest.

When he had come from the loading station Dunc had met him and hurled the time book on the packhouse floor. " Mist' Ripley, I'll be damned if I can work another lick with that old man. He's the hatefulest old man this side o' hell. You know what's he's done now. He's messed me all up with the pickin' gang, and every one of 'em aims to quit."

" It's all about Amos' watch, Katti. Amos paid three dollars and ninety-five cents for that watch in 1909. It is a fine watch. It does gain an hour once in a while, but it isn't the watch's fault. Amos says the watch is absolutely right and everybody else's watch is wrong. Amos says the pickers were an hour late this morning and he's going to get their pay docked. Poor Dunc, they all threatened to quit on him."

" Are they going to quit? "

" No, we struck a compromise. Dunc's an intelligent boy. And I told Amos, of course he was right, and they'd all have to work an hour later by his watch this afternoon."

Once in a while, I would go up to the packhouse and confer with Purdy, the packhouse boss.

" How's it coming? "

" Pretty fair. We're cullin' close to fifty percent but what goes into the crates is clean stuff."

" How about the culls today? "

" Can't seem to sell 'em at any price. They're all wormy a'course and the truck men say they can't handle 'em. They'd, most of them, ruther haul a truck back empty than cart back worms. Say, did you hear about the man who give ten bushels to a moonshiner — "

" Yes, I heard that one."

Our first real shipment, three hundred and thirty-two crates of Georgia Belles, brought two dollars a crate net and we were very much pleased.

Our next lot the American Growers sold for two dollars and fifty cents f.o.b. and we were delighted. So much so that a few days later when they told us that the buyer had made a complaint on the condition of the fruit when it arrived, and they had compromised with him by taking a cut to two dollars and thirty-five cents, we were perfectly agreeable.

The market was sagging. We knew by experience that an f.o.b. sale when no cash is paid, made at a higher price than fruit is selling for several days later when the car arrives at its destination, is hard to make stick. There are so many reasons for complaint that the buyer can trump up. The fruit is too green, or too ripe, or loosely packed.

Sometimes it's quite true that the fruit is not as it was described, and the complaint is justified and reasonable. But usually in a falling market the buyer simply feels he ought to get it for less. The American

Growers' policy seemed to be to compromise rather than sue. It was cheaper, they said, in the long run. A suit is expensive and who can prove, weeks or months after the fruit is eaten, what its condition really was when it arrived? The farmer, naturally, is the goat, for if the market rises after he has sold his car for a certain price f.o.b., he has to go ahead and ship it anyway.

Every day I studied market reports. " What I cannot see," I said to Clem, " is why the market is dropping when there are only about a third as many cars rolling as last year, not nearly so many even as in '27 when the market held up splendidly? "

There was a simple explanation. The first peaches the consumer bought in '29 were wormy. Neither Georgia or North Carolina had laws against shipping wormy stuff. A peach grower whose orchard was eaten up with worms, either had to ship worms or not ship at all. He experimented with a few cars to see if the public couldn't learn to eat worms. The housewife in New York tried another dozen peaches. She cut them open and found twelve worms. The word went 'round, " Peaches are no good this year. All I've tried are full of worms." Next time she went to market she bought cantaloupe or some other fruit.

" All that may be quite true," I insisted, when something of the sort was said to me, " but we aren't ship-

(322)

ping any wormy stuff." I remembered about that man who made the better mousetrap.

But I was told that didn't matter. Enough wormy stuff had been dumped on the market to turn people from peaches. They were leery of all peaches this season.

Our first shipment of Elbertas brought an unusual complaint. We had three hundred and thirty-two crates of Elbertas, and the rest of the car filled out with Belles. As usual, when the car reached its destination, the price had dropped below the f.o.b. sale price for which we had sold it. The buyer sent back, I believe, an entirely original kick. The Belles were all right, he said, and half the Elbertas were fine. The other half, he insisted, were not Elbertas at all.

" All I can say is," Clem told the American Growers' representative, " those trees have been Elberta trees, and borne Elbertas, for five years."

But the American Growers thought it necessary to compromise. We took a fifteen cent cut, not only on the Elbertas they claimed were off variety, but on the whole shipment, including the Belles.

We had to take a cut on nearly every shipment. The three thousand dollar profit we had looked forward to at the beginning of the season had dwindled to a scant five hundred. Instead of speaking of profit we were beginning to say, " We ought to do better than break even."

Our last car of Elbertas was might pretty.

" Grade 'em clean," said the American Growers' field man, when he came over to inspect the packhouse. " It's a fancy car sure."

Every peach that went into those crates was carefully graded and packed. The peaches had been picked over several times, and most of the wormy stuff had come off in the first pickings.

Purdy was very much pleased with the car. " I've been a packhouse boss for eight 'n ten seasons," he said, " and I don't know when I've seen a prettier car."

It rolled and we were through with packing peaches for the year. The American Growers' representative telephoned us. " Just wanted to tell you, Captain Ripley, we got two fifty f.o.b. for your car, fifty cents above the market."

" Well, that's great news," Clem said. " In spite of all the cuts we've had to take that'll give us about five hundred dollars profit above expenses."

Next day the government market report showed the market had broken to a dollar and seventy-five cents for fancy Elbertas.

" Aren't we the lucky people, though? " I crowed.

Our check came two weeks later. It was for a hundred and ninety-two dollars and two cents, a net avererage to us of less than forty-fours cents a crate.

What had happened was this: when the car reached

Hartford, its destination, the jobber had refused to accept it. The American Growers let him get away with it. They consigned it to Boston. Result, a sacrifice sale. There was nothing we could do. How can you prove what kind of peaches yours were after they've all been eaten or thrown away?

" I suppose there were several cars already in Hartford that day," Clem said, " and the buyer wouldn't take it. If farm relief would find some simple, less expensive way to enforce a contract than suing a buyer as we have to do now it would help. A case of this kind is so difficult to prove and so expensive as to be out of the question for the small grower. But I'm through," he went on. " Cured at last. It's an unbeatable game. If the market had gone up that jobber would have taken this car at two fifty. When it broke he trumped up an excuse and refused it. We've known a long time the individual grower couldn't enforce his claim, but it's taken years, and now this, to convince me that a marketing agency doesn't either. I am through."

33

We had a deficit of three hundred ninety-two dollars for the year '29. If we could have made all of our f.o.b. sales stick, we would have had a profit of about a thousand dollars in spite of the gradual decline of prices.

We knew there was no point in our continuing in the peach business. We did not want to believe that we had failed so completely and yet it was impossible to find any legitimate grower about us who could show anything but a heavy loss on his investment. This had been true for years. Many growers had lost their faith in peaches. Up and down the highway orchards were being cut down. " Nothing to peaches. Get 'em out of the way. Plant the land to something else." The Manice Orchard, the biggest in the state, two years younger than ours, was being taken out.

I thought of the time and money that had gone into

every tree that was now being cut down. I tried to say, " Yes, they're sensible not to put any more in." But it stuck in my throat. The short trunks left standing, stark and bare in the orchards, after the main tree had been hauled away, looked like grave markers in a soldiers' cemetery. " Each cut orchard is the graveyard of somebody's hopes," I thought.

The banks would no longer lend money on peach orchards. They had had to take over too many. We could only borrow on a basis of our land's value as a straight farm, that is, perhaps two or three thousand dollars.

We were forced to the conclusion that the only thing for us to do was to share-crop the farm, and hope to sell it for six or seven thousand dollars if we could, take our loss and move back to town.

There was no point in continuing to live on the farm and not run the orchard. If we did we would have to keep a man, unless Clem gave up almost his entire time to the countless small duties farm life entails: pumping water, weeding about the house, mending the two and a half miles of road between us and Samarcand, hauling and cutting fire wood, jacking up fences, and so on and on. And Clem couldn't afford the time. He must write if we were to continue to eat. If we added a farmer's wages and the upkeep of the place to our living expenses, it made living on the farm, in the midst of our abandoned orchard, more expensive than living in town.

People are always asking me, " But don't you miss your farm? Didn't you hate leaving your house, and the shrubs and trees you planted, and the road you built? "

I don't. When it was proved to be a financial failure the heart went out the place.

If you want a farm, then you want a self-supporting farm at least. Otherwise the way to enjoy the country is to have a house with either a lovely park and gardens around it, or else nature in its own wild state. A pruned, forced peach tree that grows peaches only to be dumped into the North River, or for the worms to eat, is not beautiful to me.

I loved the farm while I could believe there was a chance of its paying out, while there was a chance of the labor and the money we put into the orchard yielding us a living wage. We, and the other orchardists, would have been willing to live very simply, or to eke out the farm's return with money earned otherwise, but to work as we did, and to spend money as we did just to live on a farm and pretend we were earning a living, is all sentimental foolishness.

If the free and easy country life atmosphere that we found when we came to the Sandhills could have lasted, it would have been the ideal life. But it could not last unless the peach growers could feel that the work they were doing was worth while. Financial success is the only measure of value we have. To pour money year after year into a hopeless proposition kills the joy of endeavor, if for no other reason than it makes us feel foolish.

The simple life of planting will only support those who are willing to live like Rory and Janie, or old Amos and his sons, and often it will not even support them.

The income of this country is around ninety billion dollars and of this income only about eleven billion goes to the farmers. The proportion of the population engaged in farming is approximately twenty-five percent.

Then about one eighth of the income goes to a fourth of the population. In other words, the farmer is getting less than half what he's entitled to.

It seemed to me now that I had known for years, ever since the failure of our second honeydew crop back in '22, that we couldn't succeed at farming. It was only during that first year, when everything was new, the country, the people, the out-of-door life, that I had had faith. I had tried ever since to be optimistic, to fool myself. I had clung desperately to hope when it seemed as though our future and our whole lives must be bound up forever in the farm and peach crops. But I think I had always known.

We did not find the system of living we were looking

for when we bought the farm. It was a material system and the peach boom broke and it was gone. But we did learn something about life. Life is chance and change. Complete safety and monotony are the last things to hope for.

I don't know where the money we spent would have bought us more. The farm taught us to gamble, the pleasantest life in the world. The farm taught Clem to write adventure stories, " a good loose trade." If he'd gone to work on a newspaper in '21, he'd probably still be there with two weeks' holiday all his own out of twelve months, and a small sure salary. Farming shows you a better way. This may be the year cotton will go to forty cents. This may be the year Clem will write a best seller. There is something to look forward to — and if this should be a bad year there is always next year.

Dunc Britt, Amos' oldest boy, was anxious to share-crop the farm on halves. His wife had had pellagra. She had been better since they'd been on the place and she and Dunc liked it. Dunc was keen to risk his time and some of old Amos' and Rob's in buzzarding the trees — giving them a lick and a promise.

We traded on the following basis: if it looks like a short crop in Georgia in the spring, we advance money for fertilizer, spray and poison dust. When the season rolls 'round, we'll come up and ship the crop and give

(330)

Dunc half the net. If, however, the prospects don't look good in the spring we put out no money. Dunc can get what he can out of the crop by selling it locally to cull buyers.

The farm is still for sale at twenty cents on the dollar. But the trees are beginning to die.

A short time ago Clem and I met Charlie Bennet. Charlie Bennet, who had been Raphael's superintendent back in '22, when Clem handled the soft peaches at Samarcand. Charlie had made one or two small fortunes out of peaches and dropped them back into the peaches again.

" Well, Clem," Charlie said, " how's that boy of yours? Must be pretty near big enough to run an orchard, ain't he? "

" Well, he's pretty near big enough to run one, but I hope he has more sense," Clem said.

" Well, Cap," Charlie said, " you're right. You remember what I told you eight years ago standin' in Raphael Pumpelly's packhouse? I told you, there ain't a thing to this peach business. Any God damn fool can raise 'em and it ain't worth a damn fool's time to do it. I told you that eight years ago standin' there in Pumpelly's packhouse." He hesitated. " But I'll tell you something else, Clem. I'd rather stay here and go broke raising peaches than make a fortune not raising them. This way you get some excitement anyhow."

Two miles and a half from Samarcand, another untenanted house in the midst of a fast dying peach orchard. A little house, with roses still climbing over it and the shade trees we planted almost big enough to begin giving shade.

Charleston — deeply rooted in convention. A little golf, a little bridge. . . . And the slow rise and fall of the tides against the sea wall.

THE END.